Mrinal Pande has been the editor of *Vama* and *Saptahik Hindustan*, Executive Editor of *Hindustan Dainik*, and Senior Editorial Advisor to NDTV. She is also the founder president of the Indian Women's Press Corps. She has written extensively in Hindi and English, including novels, short stories and essays. Currently, she anchors the Hindi news for Doordarshan and writes a regular column for the *Hindu* and for *Punjab Kesari*.

Devi

✦

Tales of the Goddess in Our Time

Mrinal Pande

PENGUIN BOOKS

Penguin Books India (P) Ltd., 11 Community Centre, Panchsheel Park, New Delhi 110 017, India
Penguin Books Ltd., 27 Wrights Lane, London W8 5TZ, UK
Penguin Putnam Inc., 375 Hudson Street, New York, NY 10014, USA
Penguin Books Australia Ltd., Ringwood, Victoria, Australia
Penguin Books Canada Ltd., 10 Alcorn Avenue, Suite 300, Toronto, Ontario M4V 3B2, Canada
Penguin Books (NZ) Ltd., Cnr Rosedale and Airborne Roads, Albany, Auckland, New Zealand

First published by Penguin Books India (P) Ltd. 1996

10 9 8 7 6 5 4 3 2

Typeset in *Timpani* by Surya Computer Services, New Delhi

Made and printed in India by Swapna Printing Works Pvt. Ltd.

To my mother, from whom I learnt never to fear love or power.

To Arvind, who has helped me handle both in everyday life, without guile or guilt.

Sunahu tat yeh akath kahani,
Samujhat banat, na jai bakhani . . .

Ω   Ω   Ω

'*Listen, my dear one,*
To these indescribable tales,
Hard to follow, and still harder to narrate . . .'

(Sixteenth-century poet-saint Tulsidas)

Contents

Contents

Preface

✦

'All forms of knowledge are Thee
All women, all the world over, are Thy forms,
O Goddess!'

(Devi Mahatmya, 11:6)

In the Beginning was the Grandmother

Like every Hindu child from a conservative family, I
grew up close to the Goddesses. We met each day,
once at the beginning of the day, and once before
going to bed. We, with our hands folded in
supplication, they, their hands raised in the *abhay
mudra*, the gesture that bade us be fearless. My first
knowledge of the Goddesses derived chiefly from
my mother's mother, Ama, a small, loving, sharp-
tongued and lynx-eyed widow with many daughters,
whose chief pleasure, apart from reading Hindi
detective fiction and Gujarati poetry, lay in sitting
down each morning and evening upon her deerskin-
covered puja seat and facing the Goddesses. She
raised a huge cacophony of sounds, first with her
chants and her Tibetan brass bell, and at the later
stages, with a conch shell that she blew and blew

into. We, the girls in the house, could ignore the summons of this holy thunder only at grave peril to ourselves. So no sooner had the conch sounded, than we rushed to Ama's puja room and stood around her, with hands folded in prayer, while she rotated the *aarti* lamps in front of the deities. When she put them down, we held our palms above the flames and passed them over our faces. This ensured us good luck for the day, like the holy offering of the sweet *batasha* we received before leaving for school. A similar ritual was repeated at nightfall and compliance ensured good dreams and a sound sleep.

Our people all along the hill areas in the north, from Kashmir to Uttarakhand and Himachal, to Nepal and the North-East, have traditionally worshipped the Goddess Shakti in her diverse forms through various rituals. Grandmother's love of Goddesses, however, transcended all that. To her, as to millions of other Indian women, not only all the good but also all the bad that happened to mortals were willed by the Goddesses. True, male deities, such as Vishnu in his many incarnations and Shiva, had to co-exist in her Brahmanical pantheon, but ultimately, like the men in the family, they remained somewhat laconic, authoritarian and remote. The Goddesses were more like us. Although married to divine spouses and blessed with eternal youth, when they lost their tempers and began quarrelling, in lore and song, they seemed every bit as dreadful and artless as the neighbourhood shrews. Ever so often the Goddesses in Ama's tales also evinced a lovable vulnerability to the same illusions of *maya* that enticed mankind down below on earth, while their divine spouses observed the earthlings' sufferings detachedly. Her folk-tales and legends began at the point where Shiva and Parvati were once traversing the firmament when the divine wife saw a particularly heart-rending phenomenon down on earth. She then demanded that her all-powerful husband intervene in the lives of the miserable souls she had seen in torment, and make them happy and prosperous. The husband, like the mortal husbands and fathers we all knew, merely shrugged and made to pass on. At this, the divine spouse threw a very recognisable tantrum, shaking her head till her thick hair flew around her face, her clothes got dishevelled and her pretty face was streaked with kohl. She then stormed off and sat with her face averted, neither eating nor talking. At last the irate husband capitulated against his own better judgement, and said the magical— '*Evamastu* (So let it happen).' And with that, things changed dramatically for the affected parties.

Not always for the better, though.

If they did, how would the cycle of *karma* continue, and the labyrinthine tales of the Goddesses develop?

So the ultimate lesson to be derived was that those lovable but eternally unwise mortals would become no wiser even when redeemed by divine intervention. They would go back instead to doing things that could lose them the advantage the divine '*Evamastu*' had gained them, and at the end of their story, were capable of reverting right back to what they were initially: foolish, miserable and vain. Only for those who stood up on their own and fought back, was there some hope. And they would never beseech divine favours, only offer their thanks when they did come by them, and then move on to tackle other challenges.

♎   ♎   ♎

Narrative is the form women's knowledge of human life has taken since civilization began. The repertoire remains the same: family, penury, diligence, division, injustice, divine intervention, then back to family. The order may change, but the shape remains cyclical.

To come back to Ama's puja room and the Goddesses therein, they fell broadly into two types: the loners, and the ones with families. The loners formed a triad: Laxmi, Durga and Saraswati. The lovely Laxmi, the earthy Goddess of wealth and prosperity, was always depicted wearing a bright red silk sari bordered in gold, standing upon a lotus, showering gold coins with open palms, and being bathed with holy water from the unpraised trunks of two elephants on either side. Then there was the fearsome Goddess Durga, Mahishasur Mardini, the slayer of the buffalo demon, with her armoury of weapons held in ten hands. The demon Mahishasur had a buffalo's body and a demon's (*asura's*) head, and died at her hands, splattering blood theatrically all around. There was the Goddess Durga depicted as Simhavahini, with her wild mane and wilder looking mount, a roaring lion. She held a naked sword in one of her hands and sundry other weapons in eight others. With her tenth hand however, she blessed her devotees so that no matter how many demons she herself may be called upon to fight, her devotees would not panic.

Saraswati was the least noticeable of the triad. She was the Goddess of learning, depicted sitting on a white swan, holding a *veena*, a chisel, a string of prayer-beads, and a book. In the manner of those who patronised music and learning, she seemed haughty, remote and somewhat detached from the twin feminine spheres of domesticity and motherhood. She had no individual temple to herself in our area. She perhaps needed none.

Of the family-oriented Goddesses, one was the coy Sita, standing next to the males of her husband's family, smiling hard enough for all of them and looking, in spite of her smile, somewhat weary and drawn, as if weighed down by the enormous gold crown she had to wear for the occasion. And, of course, there was Parvati, the gutsy, talkative and playful wife of Shiva of Mount Kailas, whose family was recreated each year in Ama's house in the holy month of Shravana.

The *Dikaras*, as the divine and somewhat wild family was called, consisted of the dearly beloved wife, Parvati, her snake, animal and hemp-loving husband, Lord Shiva, and the two sons—Ganesh and Kartikeya. Parvati was squat and maternal and being a daughter of the hills, was singled out for much feasting and fussing over when the *Dikaras* were crafted out of kneaded clay by the women of the region. Parvati, like the women in our family, was fair, had a round body topped by a round moon face, and an enormous nose flanked on either side by equally enormous eyes. Her happy smile, painted on her face with a twig topped with a bit of cotton wool dipped in red *mahavar* (the varnish married women applied to their finger-and-toenails) was broad and full of good homely cheer. She had her favourite son, Ganesha, he of the elephant head, on her lap, while her handsome first-born son, Kartikeya, sat grumpily by her side. Her husband's and sons' strange familiars, a mouse, a peacock, a bull and a snake, completed the *Dikara* tableau.

And, of course, there were the clusters of sister Goddesses, the *Matrikas*, who had to be propitiated during all the festivities that marked a baby's birth. They were depicted as sixteen red dots on a hand-dyed yellow fabric and had to be felicitated with rice, milk, yogurt and roasted turmeric powder. A small bow and arrow were hung outside the door that led into the birth-room where a new mother and her male baby were quarantined for forty-two days. These objects were supposed to deter both the evil star Rahu and those sixteen fiery *Matrikas* from entering the baby's room and wreaking havoc in the form of measles, fevers, chicken-pox or other baby ailments. That it did not quite prevent the more determined ones from entering, was evident from the fact that many infants died before they left the room in the first six weeks. When a baby smiled in his sleep, it was said, with a shudder, that the *Matrikas* were tricking him into believing that they were his real mothers and that after much merry-making in his dreams the poor baby would usually wake up ill and howling. It was also said that the mischievous *Matrikas* mostly singled out male babies for such tricks, because males were more precious than females and by hurting them, the Goddesses could hurt the family more. Some clever grandmothers, who had lost several grandsons to these male-hating sisters, would dress up their new-born grandsons in girls' clothes and even put bangles on their tiny wrists, kohl in their eyes and a dot on their foreheads to simulate feminity. Female accountrements, that steadily devalued girls, were supposed to perform life-prolonging tricks for young boys.

There were also festivals all through the year when legendary good wives, like Savitri, and good daughters like Nanda and Sunanda were worshipped as Goddesses, privately within homes, and also in public on the temple premises with great fanfare. The public puja, of course, was handled entirely by males and terminated in their carrying away the Goddess-image in a palanquin to the nearby spring, where it was immersed with a great beating of drums and blowing of conch shells. It was an incredibly sad finale to a glorious homecoming, to my child's mind. But that was men's way with Goddesses and daughters.

All these Goddesses, including the lean, mean *Matrikas* and the buxom and wide-hipped *Yakshinis*, were beings of immense importance, yet infinite kindness, employing their incalculable powers towards my welfare and somehow, in spite of their vast preoccupations, willing to take a personal interest in my well-being.

As I grew up I realised also that it is as silly getting sentimental over Goddesses as over one's own mother. These are Goddesses millions of women have worshipped all their lives, sometimes for strength, sometimes for protection but mostly out of an abiding love for their own kind. One can see why. Most of us have grown up surrounded by women notably lacking in power. When we do come into adulthood, we do so, unlike young boys, with no clear understanding of what girls can achieve, but a fairly firm social mandate on what they cannot and must not aspire to be. Pushed more towards docile forms of speech and behaviour, and steered away from the world of learning, most of us have grown up feeling confused about arranging our unexpressed feelings into clear communicable thought. Stories from our times reveal how even after she's been to college, the self-control of a well-bred girl usually denies her a certain spontaneity of speech, a quickness of response and the ability to explode into good-humoured laughter. It is these qualities that the Goddesses have helped restore in our women— only to the extent it is possible, of course.

Laxmi with her frank and arrogant brushing off of fools and laggards; Parvati with her refreshing sexuality and sense of humour (she fashioned a son for herself out of body unguents and ear-wax to guard the unlatched doors of her bathing chamber), the cerebral Saraswati with her total self-absorption and her unconcealed hostility to the world of pomp and glory, are Goddesses no God can control. All of them have reopened the registers of contradictory emotions—through wit, wisdom and irony—to billions of our women, and helped them cope and fight back, win and capitulate, forget and forgive.

Our country has given cerebral deviants a strange freedom to abandon prescribed ritual. One needn't, for example, wear a headband in order to proclaim one's love for Durga, or be forced to sit in meditative fast for the nine days of Navratri. Yet one is free to experience the fierce joy and elevating warmth of reciting, even to oneself, beautiful classic verses such as the *Devi Sookta*, the *Durga Saptashati* or the *Ganga Lahari*, believing wholly in the Goddess' manifestations in those weird and wild village women, that have guarded our villages and kept them free of disease and despair when governments have not. High and low, all prostrate themselves before the Goddess as she 'appears' in the bodies of the women of lowliest castes. They ply her with food, flowers, balls of butter, kumkum and turmeric powder, offer her bangles, brassieres and saris to fulfil her desires and thereafter halt her pace so she may not rage through the village crying for more. To appease her hunger they kill goats, rams and chickens and if her tongue still lolls in her head, they offer her country-liquor that she gargles with and spews back at the people. Everyone accepts this liquor mixed with spittle as a blessing.

Millions of women, denied revenge on their tormentors, or the simple human joys of wandering away from their homes, through empty roads, swimming endlessly in mountain streams or enjoying at will the sheer lazy abandon of a get-together at temples and teashops, have sought, through closely observing these wild Goddesses and their actions, a similar untethering of secret wants, emotions and desire for creativity. One cannot, however, come by such power easily. Like Durga, all those that wish to ride a lion, must need be proud, and watchful of compromises, even if it means losing security and friends of a certain kind.

To follow the Goddesses' tales is to slip inside alphabets and go off into an uncharted territory that makes nonsense of sense as we know it.

♎   ♎   ♎

My mother, who grew up in the terribly restricted Indian upper-crust way of living in the '30s, was able to escape most of its crippling bonds with the help of circumstances that packed her off to the 'universal' poet, Rabindranath Tagore's university of Shantiniketan for over a decade. She carried around her an aura of a hard cerebral restlessness through most of my growing years. True, it set her embarrassingly apart from most women we knew; but this was what protected her undeniable talent for writing from being devoured by those voracious social mores that stood panting at the heels of all high-born women of her time. And this, her dry aloofness, helped her realize her artistic potential in a way few Indian women of her generation have. She wrote, she broadcast, she brought literature and music into our lives (shrugging aside all loudly uttered fears about both making women 'cheap'). She saw to it that we, her daughters, read and heard the best there was, even if it meant our going without the necessary apprenticeship to housekeeping, and winning friends and influencing people in the father-in-law's house.

In the manner of many daughters, we were not terribly supportive of Mother initially. Memory also tells me that we were frequently discomfited by her persistence and occasionally even rather fretful and bored. But today we, her daughters, are enormously grateful to her for what I now perceive as a rare gift of a great and abiding love for the Goddess in ourselves. I remember when I was a precocious and highly-strung ten, and always getting into bitter and embarrassing arguments with family elders and playmates, subsequently having nightmares each night and waking up the babies with my terrified and feverish shrieks, Mother introduced me to the Goddess-tales from the *Markandeya Purana* and to the *Devi Kavach*, a cluster of verses known literally as 'the divine armour'. I was to recite the Sanskrit couplets aloud, read the meaning given below in Hindi, and then put the holy book under my pillow to soothe my anguished sleep. It worked somehow, during the sleeping hours at least. My waking hours continued to be somewhat chaotic and cantankerous though, because in domestic matters Mother was not a great housekeeper or a patient and diplomatic problem-solver.

Once I began my own long forays into the world of the printed word, I was to relearn that language or *Vac*, is a form of Saraswati, the Goddess of learning. She is the one that has sprung the lock for millions of women, like my mother and myself, and helped minds leap away from the fearful prisons of silence. To meditate on the Goddess' names is to find in the natural phenomena around us—our rivers, seas, mountains (each of which is named after one of her manifestations)—the compasses to guide those difficult journeys to unknown lands. To follow the tales about the nine Durgas, the ten *Bhairavis*, the sixteen *Matrikas*, or the numerous *Gram Devis* or village Goddesses, is to rediscover countless pathways hidden around ourselves. There is also that conjuction when mind meets mind in a space that is totally free, and we can begin to see tales from our own time reflected in the pool of timeless stories.

Discoveries such as these, and other things, conspired to make me in later life both a writer and a journalist. But ironically, when I first became a journalist, Mother was alarmed. She thought I would not be fulfilling thus either my duties as wife and mother, or my own potential as an artist and writer. For a time I was aware that I frightened her as I replayed many of her experiences in my own life: bulldozing my way into one male preserve after another, speaking my mind, alienating bosses, relatives and friends and earning an unfemininely handsome salary.

Like my mother, I have survived even as Scheherezade had survived, also the thirty-two fairies of the *Dwatringsha Puttalika* stories, cursed with the responsibility to shoulder and guard King Vikramaditya's throne of Truth. We all escaped to our freedom with the help of the stories we created and recited, notwithstanding the distractions around us.

Or perhaps it is the distractions that gave us our ability to locate and string the tales together. Who knows? All we know is that the Goddess-tales lean towards human tales. They soak each other up.

These days, with my daughters grown up and gone far away in pursuit of their own careers, I go through my days wondering exactly like Mother, what will happen in our terribly mobile lives next? Will my daughters at some point be able to shake off this fearsome legacy of a duty to settle down, and be like everyone else? Or will I one day get a sudden letter or phone call, informing me of a major decision they have taken, or not been able to take because they are my daughters. There will be principles involved in their decisions that I may understand little of and Mother even less. Yet we know that our decisions may somewhere be interlinked. It is an acute agony that strikes all independent women of our times, mostly in the middle of the night, when the body may be at rest, but the mind is free to wander.

At recurring points in our lives, we all want to move, only we do not know how to judge things and directions. We desperately need a structure against which to measure things for ourselves, a context into which we can fit deviant human behaviour including our own. And yes, there are times when we find it hard to live with the extremes of feelings within us that are ripping us apart, yet of which we understand so little:

> *Sunahu tat yeh akath kahani*
> *Samujhat banat, na jai bakhani.*

> 'Listen, my dear one,
> To these indescribable tales,
> Hard to follow, and still harder to narrate.'

Goddess-tales, all the tellers will tell you, are ever-changing. They can never be encountered in the same shape twice. Some read or sound better than the others, some are barely received, some we forget no sooner than they've been recounted, only to have them swim up one night as the mind flows with the currents of insomnia.

> *Sunahu tat yeh akath kahani . . .*

Indescribable tales that travel in small groups.

Tales of women behind closed doors, women weeping quietly, women walking down endless roads and forests, women laughing out loud. Women sighting the Goddess. Women whom the Goddess' spirit has entered. To recount their tales is to move into mysterious grey cremation grounds littered with the half-burnt bones of generations. It means stepping into the timeless kingdom of Mahakali and the Nine Durgas, there to tick like mad clocks, striking minutes and hours off time.

Shailputri, she who is the defiant daughter of the

mountains, Brahmacharini, the loner, who has chosen to be a celibate, Chandraghanta, she who wears the moon round her neck, Kooshmanda, she who is the warmth of the ova within the womb, Skandmata, the mother of Skanda the warrior, Katyayani, who has slain fearsome demons like Katyayan, Kalratri, who is the dark destructive Goddess of the final night of Navratri, Mahagauri, the fairest of them all, and ultimately, Siddhidatri, the giver of the ultimate boon.

> '*When being consumed by fires; when in the midst of a battle among enemies, facing a tough, hard and lonely journey, scared and confused, we turn to Thee, to remove the impediments and set us free to move . . .*'

(Durga-Saptashati)

Ω   Ω   Ω

For Indian women, Goddesses have always been there, normal and magical at the same time. They learn from them all the time. Without knowing it, of course.

Men have eternally tried to convince the Goddesses that they too are their worshippers and so the divine beings must come to them as loyal and gentle mothers. Since few Goddesses have children, in their secret wishes men want to take their children's place and so reinvent the perfect mother, wild and fierce, yet loyal and all-pardoning.

Strange tales are being used like tools to hammer and carve the Goddesses into mothers of men. Grimly, steadily, almost ritually, these tales are replacing the real legends. Loudspeakers play raucous modern songs sung by the sons of Mata—a benign mother of men, enthroned in the house, steady as a rock. Day and night, television and films wring away the life from sublime stories to fashion serials around this Mother Goddess, as testaments to the transferring powers of men and money. Here, Goddesses are presented through word and image as overdressed, bejewelled and fawning mothers, givers of wealth and gentle imposers of discipline. Those unpredictable outbursts of temper, that fury of wild hair, those rolling eyes, the lolling tongue and other manifestations of an inexplicably complex presence, are all being erased from Goddess-lore. One hears songs that ask the Mata to come to Bharat and slay the infidels, to present worshippers with houses with marble floors, to help the daughters-in-law bear only sons, to help businesses prosper and daughters get married early to suitable boys.

We, the tellers of tales, are sardonic witnesses to this sly coming together, in the name of the Mother, of the land-grabbing urban householder, the corrupt rural farmer, the oily politician and his supporters in the gutter press. They wait to find a gap in the tales, then rush in to substitute the fake for the authentic.

And we, the writers and narrators of tales, have nothing else to guide us out of this swirling fog of lies, except a certain restlessness in our bones that we translate into language.

Move. Move. Move, the stories say.

Move. Move. Move, says the Goddess.

Then one day, we sit down and begin to write.

We write of all that has been happening and also of all that which will no longer happen. We write of our mothers cooking, cleaning and swabbing with a timeless vitality. We write of fathers with their voices raised in command. We write of the rituals we saw and religious tales we heard as children. We write of the first sly sightings of adolescent hairs and the fragrance of the *garbhagriha*, the womb-rooms of the temples. We write of the smell of a woman lusting for a man. We write of homes that have no men and children. We write of children that are yet to be conceived.

We write of men, powerful, handsome and attractive.

We write of men, mean, vengeful and repellent.

We write of women fulfilled and happy.

We write of women betrayed.

We write of women who, when they've had enough, lift their ravaged faces to the moon and bay like she-wolves.

We write of men who give an answering call.

We write of the years gone by and years to come, and of the No-Man's-Land that borders the inner spaces of all mankind, where men, women and children hurl about like meteorites.

Welcome to the world of Goddesses.

The Warrior Goddess

In an age of deadlines, it is obvious that one must first make a beginning and that the beginning must' lead to an end. And that together they must move in time.

The problem is, how and where do you begin the story of the great Goddess, Mahadevi, who danced upon the prostrate body of Kala, the lord of time?

And if you resolve that somehow, in what language do you go on to describe one who is also Vac Devi, the mother of all speech, who is said to pare all flesh off language and fling it like a necklace of bones casually around her neck?

In what frame of context may you place one who questions all the existing frames, and who, when you look to her for a firm explanation, sticks out an enormous red tongue and moves on?

Just moves on.
Like the stories.

Ω   Ω   Ω

Our times.

Scenes all over the world are at once fantastic and familiar. Men, women and children gone truant, outside their tribe. Lost, savage and sinful. But also alive, free and fighting fit.

December 19, 1994: A somewhat cold day in the capital of India. There is smoke from woodfires, smoke from hundreds of chimneys that belong to illegal factories in and around the city. It's a Monday, and the world seems to be in a state of turmoil. In New Delhi, the Congress Party is crumbling; in the Chechen Republic, Russian planes and tanks are raining death and destruction on the people of Grozny. In Karachi, militant Sunnis are gunning for Shias, and in Europe, Serbs and Bosnian Muslims have set out to destroy each other to the last speck of life.

Ω   Ω   Ω

On the Indo-Nepal border, one Phool Kumari (literally the 'flower-virgin'), a sixteen-year-old aboriginal girl, is abducted by a group of goons. When she cannot fob off this group of drunkards, who are out to gang-rape her, she bites off the member of the leader of the gang. The bitten man turns out to be a Member of the Legislative Assembly of Bihar, and his gleeful politician opponents see to it that he is expelled from his party and put into jail.

In the Caucasian mountains, old Chechen women dance in front of a BBC camera. A beautiful blonde tells us in a clipped British accent that they are clapping their hands to keep up the 'national spirit'.

The Russians bombs rain down.

♎   ♎   ♎

'What do we need voter identity cards for?' the grandmotherly woman of Shekhadi, Shamsoonisa, asks journalist Kalpana Sharma. 'I know who I am. I know that I live here. What do I need to prove? If I wanted to go abroad I would need a passport. But why do I need an ID card? Suppose I decide I do not want to vote?' The locals tell Kalpana, she, Shamsoonisa, is mad.

♎   ♎   ♎

On January 11, 1995, one K.P. Valsala Kumari becomes the first woman in the age group of ten to fifty allowed to visit the Sabarimala Ayyappan Temple in Kerala. She was permitted by the Kerala High Court on December 7, 1994 to do so, to oversee civic amenities as an administrator.

Since 1990, the issue of possibly menstruating women entering the hallowed portals of the celibate deity's temple has been hotly debated in the state of Kerala. After a court order supporting the ban, lady doctors, policewomen and the Devasom guards of the temple were posted at vantage points to stop the entry of women pilgrims who could not furnish proof of not belonging to the ten to fifty age group.

The courts however did not allow Valsala to climb

the ultimate hallowed flight of eighteen steps (*Pathinettam padi*) and meet the celibate deity Ayyappan face to face.

℩   ℩   ℩

One thing becomes slowly clear. From no matter which point one chooses to begin the tales about the Goddess, the point of entry will always be mobile, always arbitrary, and always fitted against a backdrop of shifting norms and merging colours; also always full of unusual combinations: power and powerlessness, victory and loss, birth and death, laughter and pain.

℩   ℩   ℩

1995: Saturn and Mars have moved close to each other. Even the combination of Ma Usha Prem's tarot cards, in the glossy Sunday supplement, shows Moon, Magus, and the Queen of Swords, suggesting illusion and destruction followed by rebuilding. Icy breezes blow from the snow-covered Himalayan mountains in the north down towards Delhi. The temperatures are plummeting as women in the mountains of Uttarakhand sit on night-long, day-long *dharnas* to protest against police atrocities on their folk. They have shut and padlocked all schools, office buildings, and the district collector's *kachheri*. They have refused to submit to condoning firings, baton-charges and the rape of local women by the state police.

Strange, isn't it, that the chief minister of the state is called Mulayam Singh. Literally translated, the name means the 'soft lion'. His aim is to restore social justice and those hillfolk who defy him shall be thrashed by men from the plains. He says the women and the media always exaggerate things and need to be pulled up. His men fan out to beat up both. Editors complain but are silenced. The women however say they'll not bring him and his government down. They heckle men and media who try to warn them.

Go hide behind your wives' skirts, the women say to them, and laugh so hard that tears spring in their eyes.

♎ ♎ ♎

It suddenly strikes me that the first name of the Goddess is Shailputri, daughter of the mountains. Slowly, first the political parties, and then the dailies, begin to support a form of social justice that replaces bullies of one caste with another. But the voices of the hillwomen ring out loud and clear like the Panchdhatu temple bells, against cant, against duplicity.

Shailputri could not be far away. She, who destroyed even her own father, Daksha, when he chose to be unjust and unkind.

♎ ♎ ♎

Faxes pile on editorial tables like entrails. Disasters. Exodus. Civil wars. Refugees. Firings. Rallies. Resistance. Rape.

A dark aura, the collective rage of Shailputri's female followers, begins to emanate from the eight hill districts of Uttarakhand, as reporters cover their eyes and editors choke, women's rage fills the skies. Fear—of men, of open roads, dark fields, the police, the CBI, the PAC—ceases to matter. Anger crackles like newsprint.

♎   ♎   ♎

Then the darkness passes slowly over to the plains, usurping power from all the ruling parties one by one. As it fills the citadels of power, the usually disdainful and chattering voices in the Legislative Assemblies and the corridors of the Secretariat begin to shake. A little at first, then more, when something seems to topple and fall through the air. The aura moves among the lush green southern plains of Karnataka, of Andhra Pradesh. It turns over and over like the rotating blades of Vishnu's deadly *chakra* and also slashes up another state government up around the north-eastern mountains.

♎   ♎   ♎

The dark arrogance of the ruling powers begins to come apart. Gujarat. Maharashtra. Orissa. Andhra Pradesh. Karnataka.

The 'Anti-Incumbency Factor', our wise men of the media term it. The women laugh. They know better. Alone and unsupported they have reached out to men and women all over the land. A collective rage now hangs over the entire country like a turbulent black cloud that will not go away. Thousands of eyes scan the centre of the government with scornful rancour.

☊   ☊   ☊

May 1995: Mulayam Singh's government is toppled by a woman from the erstwhile untouchable caste. Women ululate across slate-covered roofs as the news passes from rooftop to rooftop. The Goddess has arrived with an angry cry of '*Hoonkar!*' She shall not hesitate to topple even this government, should it turn demonic.

☊   ☊   ☊

Women in the mountains run their eyes now beyond the horizon, where the plains lie. This is where the battle must now be carried to. It is time things were torn down and rearranged.

Time that the battle moved to the plains.

☊   ☊   ☊

'*It is I who move about as the Rudras,*
It is I who am the Adityas and all other Gods.
I am the one that supports Mitra and Varuna.
Indra and Agni and the twin Ashwins too.
I am the power behind the powers
Of Soma, Twashtri, Pushan and Bhaga,
And it is I who bestow wealth and consciousness
On all who perform the sacrifice and bring offerings.

I am the sovereign power, the bestower of all wealth
I am the first to be offered a sacrifice
The Gods, wherever they be, worship me,
Who am of many forms and present everywhere.
Whosoever eats, sees, breathes or hears what is spoken
Does it through me, I, who am of many forms.
Those who do not know this, shall perish.
Listen to me, O worthies; what I say can be understood
Only with faith and reverence.
This truth that I tell ye is respected by gods and men.
Whom I will, I mark with greatness.
Whom I will, I make into a creator,
Into a seer, a genius.
I bend the bow of the Rudras to slay the enemy of the wise ones
I wage wars to protect the good.
I cover the heaven and earth and I
Am the one that gives birth to this expanse of universe.
I was born of deep waters and permeate the various worlds,
My body touches the heavens above.
I roar as the wind creating the universe. As I blow,
I transcend the heavens above and the earth below.
This, know ye, is Me.'

(125th hymn, 10th Mandala)

As Vac, the daughter of the sage Ambhrana, sat meditating on the banks of the river Saraswati, she had a vision of the Goddess. It was this vision that metamorphosed into the beautiful hymn.

Women shall always see the Goddess first.

Through Vac's timeless poem, the great Goddess emerges first as the transcendent supreme Shakti, a powerful and limitless consciousness. She then sets into motion millions of forces that create the coiled sphere of power. Out of this, when the time comes, Shakti re-forms herself as countless Goddess-shapes, and when the battle is over, the shapes re-enter the sphere one by one and lie coiled. Waiting.

So also the Goddess tales.

The pool is Shakti.

'*All women everywhere in the world, are thy forms O Goddess.*' Thus says the *Markandeya Purana* whose thirteen chapters (*Chapters 81 to 93*) are today regarded as the most sacred text of the Shaktis, or worshippers of Shakti. To this is added the *Devi Kavacha*, appended to the *Chandi*, that merges nine more forms of the Devi along with their nine mothers. Blood-thirsty Goddesses like Chamunda and Katyayani too enter the group. They could have graced a warrior clan as the Goddess Kaushiki graced that of the Kaushikas. They are joined by the contemplative Buddhist Goddesses, Tara and Chinnamasta (Vajrayogini), who in later lore begin to bare their fangs.

Battles are the occasions that cause waves in the brackish waters of the extraordinary pool, and one by one the Goddesses emerge, to challenge the forces of destruction.

So do the tales.

♎   ♎   ♎

Goddess tales are told and retold in Hindu houses, mostly during festivals. And for us who were born and raised in the hills of the Uttarakhand, each festive occasion began with a puja performed for the three great Goddesses—Maha Laxmi, Maha Kali and Maha Saraswati, locally called the *Jyoontis*.

These three identical Goddess-figures were to be drawn on paper and then coloured in with great care by the daughters of the house, unmarried or otherwise.

The *Jyoontis* or *Jeeva Matrikas* (mothers of all living creatures) correspond exactly to the great male triad of deities, Brahma, Vishnu and Mahesh. For us, these *Jyoontis* together formed a divine crucible of power, from which all Goddess-tales took their initial spin. We were told that originally there was but one Goddess, Maha Devi, created out of a merger of the gaze of the great male triad, as they sat planning the destruction of the demon Andhaka (darkness), he of a thousand arms who pretended he was blind, but in fact was not.

However, in the way of all creators, once the Goddess arrived, all the three wanted to possess her. At this, like all women faced with the pulls and counterpulls of the family, the Mahadevi is said to have smiled and split her divine self in three. The Goddess now metamorphosed into three incarnations: Maha Saraswati, Maha Laxmi and Maha Shakti or Maha Kali. Each of these, like the three great male gods, represented one of the basic *Tatwas*, or mindsets: Saraswati symbolised the *Sattwa* (represented by the colour white, signifying the purity in which all colours merge), Laxmi, the *Rajas* (represented by the colour red, signifying life) and Kali, the *Tamas* (represented by black, signifying darkness).

♎   ♎   ♎

The great Goddess is mercurial, authoritative and insubordinate. She is so because the power of powers, and the leader of leaders cannot be otherwise. Even though the male Gods were armed with greater authority and decisive powers, Maha Shakti's mercurial wanderings in and out of the established pantheon were to remain a source of awe and anxiety. To tame the situation and curb her, stories were invented around her that accentuated her maternal and wifely aspects, but the threads of the Gauri-Parvati, Laxmi and Durga fables began to tense with a power of their own and those who spun those threads stepped back in terror.

Euphemistic interpretations were to have about as much limiting effect on the Goddess, as the banks of a river in high spate. Movement and freedom are central to all her forms.

'It is I who move about as the Rudras . . .'

And her access to time and freedom of movement in space become her two most perfect levers of power. Those who are powerless, are so precisely because they have neither the time nor the mobility: to plan, to strategize, to fight back and gain and regain lost power and then to structure it around one's desire.

'I bend the bow of the Rudras to slay the enemy . . .'

No, the Goddess is not a static glow. Never. As she enters battle, she is more like a meteor, free of all gravitational pulls and counterpulls, of the need to keep to a given stellar role. Thus the name Ulka Devi. There are, in fact, two temples to Ulka Devi—the meteor Goddess—in the town of Almora in the Himalayan foothills. As children we often found little porous stones in our orchards, that we were told were meteorites. We called them *tara-goo*, star-turd. Folding your hands and invoking Ulka Devi was said to protect you from falling star-turds.

♎   ♎   ♎

Whether a meteor or a protector from falling stars, the Goddess continues to be a natural wanderer and a leader of all those who share her sense of delightful irony, who love challenges and have themselves challenged established authority. Thus over centuries bandits and prostitutes, astrologers and practitioners of black magic, witches and excrement and flesh-eating Kapaliks, have all become her devotees. They gravitate to her effortlessly as a calf seeks his mother's udders.

All these precarious out-groups in society who wished to break out of the deadly and leaden monotony of their given space in the caste and class ladder, all those individuals and sects with hidden desires and secret practices, become pre-destined to follow the Goddess' path. That the calf follows its mother home is a law of nature.

To meditate upon the various forms that the Goddess takes, is to enter a precarious and ambiguous cycle of moral and intellectual nomadism; a world without a fixed address, full of stars and star-turds, shiftings and migrations, in short, a land of visions, hallucinations, fear, laughter, and of course, tales.

Ω   Ω   Ω

The tales about the warrior Goddess, like the protagonist herself, never try to bring order into the normal chaos of life. They help, rather, to put in order one's own understanding and perceptions about chaos, and thus also about ourselves. The logic of Goddess-tales is not a logic of references, but a release from it.

'*As I blow, I transcend the heavens above and earth below . . .*'

A virtual ocean of such Devi tales surges around us; always full of random movement and mobile shadows. Much like the Goddess herself. It is entirely possible that as one lunges to grab for one constant meaning, the tales shall move on, suddenly scattering the fragmented incidents like so many pieces of a broken mirror; or star-turds.

♎   ♎   ♎

The demon Andhaka is on a rampage.

The three great gods sit confabulating. Dour. Circumspect. Virtuous. And cold. There are whispers of defeated alliances, treacheries, secret treaties. Rumours fly around like monsoon gnats: debacles, carnage, slaughter. The Gods are worried. Very worried. This demon is proving to be too tricky, too mobile, too adept at changing himself. The occasion calls for a superior power of the sort they only possess in portions. He has to be destroyed by a sublime power that challenges the demon's dark arrogance while its own appearance carries no hint of the real ingenuity, cunning and indomitable courage within.

In short, a female warrior.

Yes. They decide they shall call upon their inner powers to arise and meet and metamorphose into a supreme deity.

They begin to meditate.

The Gods don't have much to discuss generally, except when a catastrophe of some magnitude brings them together, but over time they have developed a certain camaraderie. Do they not carry scars from the same battles? And have their eyes not been witness to the same devastations? Today they offer their fire, their potency, and their weapons jointly, to One who shall be neither submissive nor subordinate. One who shall not give but take from them, their fire, their strength, their potency.

They meditate. Their words of worship and sacrifice to the Great She, when uttered, take off like so many neutrons. Slowly, the words go on to become part of the general renewal of strange nomadic lore. Hers is to be a literature that shall move against all literary norms of time and space. Vama, they call the Goddess. She who moves on the left, on the side of the jackals, and death. The grammarian Vopdesha pauses to remind us, however, that Vama is also beauty. She who moves in beauty.

Strange name, Vama. Even in mathematics, the Vama method of calculation is radically different from the normal one. In it, the numbers jump up and down, move sideways and multiply with a furious speed.

Other names are no less fascinating: Ulka Devi, the meteor-Goddess, a terrible perfection of a beauty who plots her own wild and blazing migrations. Bhramari Devi, the queen-bee, who shall drink nectar and buzz around darkly pollinating Creation, heavy with honey and the heady fragrance of blossoms.

The eyes of the Gods meet. Their gazes merge.

In a burst of indescribably powerful light, the great Goddess descends. She arrives not gently, but with a roar that shakes the three worlds.

The Gods bow low—'May you conquer all O Goddess!'

Silence.

The Goddess watches the army of the demon with wild, blood-shot eyes.

Chikshur, Chamar, Udagra, Mahahanu, Bashkal, Parivarit, Bidal, and among them their leader, the demon Mahishasur, pawing the earth like a wild buffalo.

Buzzards are beginning to circle above.

Silence.

The mountains capped with snow are bristling

with conifers. There are enormous opportunities for ambush and for a prolonged war that shall gather force and then fan out as it moves down to the plains. If she, the Goddess, leads into the battle, the battlefield must also move.

The Goddess is armed. She bears weapons offered her by the Gods: the *khetak, tomar, parashu, pash, trishul* and *chakra*. She has strung them together and casually wears some around her neck, others she holds in her many arms. Some are strapped around her strong life-bearing hips.

The tricky buffalo demon tries the usual ruse. 'What is a pretty woman like you doing on the battlefield?' he croons and disappears with a laugh. The Goddess glares. She knows all about male illusions. As the army of demons comes rushing to her, the Goddess twangs her bow. Her lions roars.

The Gods cower in waiting.

Together the Goddess and her mount set out to decimate the demon army. What follows is butchery. Feet slither in blood and mouths utter animal sounds as power is pitted against power.

From the body of the Goddess, a whole retinue begins to emerge. Ambika—who roars like a forest fire through the demon ranks. The Ganas— misshappen souls who dance and kill and dance again. Ishwari—she, of the three eyes, flourishing a trident.

And then she, Mahadevi, the great Goddess, utters a most fearsome battle cry. The great baleful roar of someone fiercely angry and eager to let the enemy know it.

'Where are you?'

Echoes multiply: 'Are you, are you, are you . . .'

The demon materializes as a buffalo. He bellows 'Umbhaaaah . . .' as though flood waters were surging out of a cave.

A buffalo deserves treatment befitting a buffalo.

The Goddess throws her *pash* over him and as the noose tightens, the buffalo turns first into a demon, then into an elephant and then again into a buffalo, pawing the earth, inviting, daring the woman riding a lion to lift her hand against him.

The Goddess is in no hurry. She looks at a companion-in-war who hands her a cup of gold, brimful of wine.

This is some war!

The Goddess takes a long swallow and begins to laugh. Her eyes are red as she wipes a pink palm across her mouth. Then holding the demon beneath her feet, she slowly lifts her dark arm. With one blow she severs his head. She strikes again and again, and hacks away piece after piece of the hard rubbery buffalo hide. The great lidless demon eyes cloud over with death. The demon collapses.

The Goddess laughs.

♎   ♎   ♎

The battle is over, so also the ritual paeans to the great commander who has taught Gods to be Gods, cowards to fear and the compassionate to weep. The Gods now wish to be left alone, but they are too awed to ask the Goddess to leave. They look at each other.

Silence.

'Ask for a boon,' booms the Goddess. She is enjoying this.

'Please come whenever there is trouble O Goddess,' the Gods stammer out.

'So be it.'

The Goddess laughs a drunk and crooked laugh. She knows.

The Gods hold their breath.

The Goddess departs.
Silence trembles for a long time after her, like the blades of the *doorva* grass.

The Shailputri

In the beautiful hill resort of Nainital, there is by the side of a lake, an old temple of the Goddess Naina Devi. She is the one the town is named after. Legend has it that the temple was built to mark the site where the eyes (*nain*) of Sati, the wife of Shiva, fell as her corpse was slowly dismembered by Vishnu's *chakra*. Sati's eyes, marked on a black stone, have been worshipped as Naina Devi by millions of hillfolk through the centuries.

Sati, the daughter of the arrogant king Daksha, had married her beloved, the ascetic Shiva, much against her aristocratic family's wishes. Once, when the father was preparing to hold a major *yagya*, he deliberately chose not to invite Shiva, who with his dishevelled appearance and eccentric retinue, he deemed a source of social embarrassment. Sati heard of the great event in her father's house and begged her husband to let her go, even if he didn't. When Shiva refused, Sati threw a most fearsome tantrum, once again generating a whole army of companions-in-war from her body. Together they shrieked and stamped their furious feet till permission was granted.

Shiva watched Sati go, with sad eyes.

It was a disastrous homecoming for Sati.

Upon reaching her father's house, she realized

why her wise consort had refused to come. Daksha was cold and rude to his daughter and also said the most insulting things about her husband and female companions, as the family watched in silence with unconcealed hostility. No one welcomed her. Everyone joined to wait for her humiliation to be complete. The irate Sati proceeded to curse and curse such coarse behaviour and finally immolated herself on the sacrificial fires.

When the news of the death of his wife reached Shiva, he arrived at the scene, put what remained of Sati's body upon his shoulders, uttered a great cry of grief and went on a most fearsome rampage, destroying everything within sight. The Gods rushed to Vishnu, to help stop the divine ascetic from destroying the universe. As Shiva rampaged through the three worlds, Vishnu proceeded to cut off portions of Sati's body with his *Sudershan chakra* into fifty-one pieces. As the body disappeared, Shiva's great grief abated somewhat and thus the universe, they say, was saved from total annihilation.

Sati dotted the land thereafter.

The spots where the parts of Sati's body fell came to be known as *peeths* or sacred spots.

Like all good stories, the story of Sati's life and death acquires meanings as it rolls on, and the fifty-one *peeths* become fifty-one lexicons, not only for those that seek solace but also for those that do not need to.

As a young girl I visited the Naina Devi temple often, with the women of the family, or all by myself, drawn by the sheer magnetism of the eyes of the Goddess. The eyes made one hesitate. Her gaze was intimidating. It had a kind of arrogance. No, it was not arrogance, but the granite-hard honesty of one who does not suffer fools gladly, not even her father. She observed, listened and, one felt, at the same time somehow rearranged within her what she saw and heard, extracting from it a sense beyond the comprehension of those with ordinary minds. She knew, I was sure, what it feels like to a girl, to be humiliated for the company she keeps, to be ostracized and left out in the cold for daring to be different from her sisters, by people she was raised to love and trust.

♎   ♎   ♎

There are forgeries here too. And clever ones.

'Sati Mata' they came to call women who we know were often drugged and dragged to their husband's pyres and burnt to a cinder, so the family would not have to worry about looking after a young widow. The rising heat of passion still influences the Sati-worshippers, as they remember the good old days when you asked a woman to die and she did. 'You city-women with your Western education, you know nothing about our long tradition,' the minister wearing a saffron turban shouts at us.

With a little coaxing and expunging the word 'sati' has been made to denote all those women who expired on their husbands' pyres, out of sheer love. Scions of major business-houses still send their daughters-in-law on pilgrimages to temples their families have built to Sati Mothers.

Thus do stars become star-turds.

Deliver us from such star-turds, O Ulka Devi.

♎   ♎   ♎

Sati's tale not only does not carry the implications mostly associated with the word today, it also questions many other concepts in which Indian women are raised to believe. Sati's death is only in part about a wife's loyalty to her husband. Mostly it is about how worldly considerations may invert accustomed relationships between humans, between father and daughter, between sisters and even between husband and wife. Sati is tough meat. No wonder most householders worship Sati only after her reincarnation as Parvati, a girl in whom the story of Sati's life acquires a happily reconciliatory ending. As foster-mother of sons, Skanda and Ganesh, Parvati is transformed into a kind, maternal woman, who visits her father's house each year in her full glory. She is received and sent off as an honoured guest. They make sure she does not leave her father's house in a fiery choking ball of smoke, but is carried on shoulders in a palanquin to be immersed gently with a beating of drums and blowing of conches. She is immersed in the ever-nourishing waters of a river with traditional words of affectionate farewell—'Come again Mother!'

Perhaps we urban worshippers, unlike the villagers, are reluctant to face the dire implications of the dark death of Sati. But make no mistake. Several tales reveal how Parvati too carries within her all of Durga's fierce combative powers. The *Linga Purana* tells the tale of how our gentle Parvati killed the demon Daruka, at a request from her husband. She is said to have entered Shiva's body and partaken of the poison stored within his blue throat. As she drank the poison, once again her fair form took on a dark colouring and with a fierce cry she changed from Gauri (fair one) into a warrior Goddess with a mottled face called Kali (the dark one).

The Tale of Vijaya

It was a bad parting. A sad farewell.

The last I saw of Vijaya was when her lifeless body, swathed in a white sheet, was being wheeled away in a gently rattling trolley from her apartment to the elevator, to the ambulance, to the morgue, where, as her five-year-old-son told my three-year-old-daughter, the doctor would cut her open like a brinjal. A hand had escaped the sheet as the trolley turned the corner. The arm was bent at the elbow, the hand raised as though in farewell.

Vijaya was only thirty years old. She had lived in the USA for ten years and never been home to Kerala from where she came as a newly-wed, during that period. Her husband, a plump, dark-skinned and jolly man, seemed a harmless and gentle fellow and was much given to smiling at all the residents of the apartment building, no matter whether he knew them or not.

Vijaya and I lived on the same floor and since we had both come from India as young, clueless wives, and had children of about the same age, we met often in the home and playground and washed, fed and fretted over our babies and our futures together. In the manner of all young expatriate Hindu wives, once we had seen the husbands off to work, we sat and chatted about this, that and the other while also keeping a vigilant and indulgent eye on our offspring.

Mostly we talked about our lost natal homes, and how different this land was, how hostile. I told Vijaya the resident snoop Diane had told me that she and her friends had observed that we were the only two mothers frequenting the sandbox who never said to their children, 'I'll kill you!' through clenched teeth.

'*Ayyo!* Why should we say that?' Vijaya had

laughed her throaty peasant laugh. ' "Kill, kill, kill!" that is all these people say, all the time!'

Vijaya spoke a twangy, nasal American. Unlike mine, her English had a pure American accent because she had picked it up after she came to Washington.

She had been through a tough patch initially, she told me. Her husband was a student during their early years and money was always short. He taught her English and she began doing odd jobs, often working eighteen hours a day. It was a humiliating life she said, when her employees often talked about her as though she was mentally deficient or just not there. She cried each night in her husband's arms, who told her through clenched teeth to bear up some more. Now he had a green card and a good job and she had a son. But Vijaya never quite shook off her rage, in spite of the fact that she was a trusting woman in the manner of a rural girl who had put herself together with her husband's help, and had an unshakeable confidence in his ability to cope. She would barge into my apartment, head for the living room, sit on the edge of her favourite chair, and start chatting, totally disregarding my natural diffidence. Unlike me she was spontaneous and devastating in her observations about the men and women around us.

I was occasionally embarrassed by her dominating ways in the playground where she shielded our offspring and their playthings from the naturally aggressive American children like a dragon. But she told me that that, her husband said, was the only way to fob off the 'foreigners'. They'd grab everything from our children, otherwise, she said, we must fight back.

She knew all about salesgirls too.

When we went shopping and one of them refused to go and look for something we needed, Vijaya would browbeat the hapless girl, shouting at her till her nerve broke, and I would suffer with the girl. At such times her face would change colour, her eyes grow bloodshot and she'd fairly crackle with fury. As we returned home, however, she'd suddenly regain her calm confidence and her natural colouring, and was once again loving and jolly, as we took the elevator upstairs.

The same Vijaya was gone.

She had killed herself suddenly, for no apparent reason.

A few hours before her suicide, she had come to me to borrow an electric iron as hers was not working. 'I feel so unwanted,' she had said to me as she departed, with a faint smile, which was perhaps not a smile at all, but an attempt at swallowing a great grief. I had a vague notion that her husband had taken to heavy drinking. Once she came to the playground with a black eye, but I said nothing to her. My urban Hindu upbringing forbade such obvious probings into others' lives.

The autopsy was conclusive. It was a suicide, the husband said, as he collected his bewildered son from my apartment. He thanked me and I thanked him as usual for letting my daughter have his son's company for the day, pretending it was all a joke and that Vijaya was back there in the apartment waiting for her son with cookies and milk, with a smile as big as the Dwitiya moon.

$$\Omega \qquad \Omega \qquad \Omega$$

Vijaya was gone. Her sturdy peasant's body, nourished on cow's milk and home-made butter and baskets full of fruit, had not stood a chance against the black wave of her deep self-destructive rage.

Presumably she had been hinting at her dark anger with words and gestures we couldn't quite put a meaning to. The exact pathology of her fury was something that would always elude our sensible worlds, although our cookies too were frequently crumbling, and our pots of milk boiling and boiling over till nothing was left, except a charred skin that crumbled on touch.

Black is a terribly persistent colour.

It dots the landscape even after the body is gone.

Mother's Dussera

'We went to the Nanda Devi temple on Dussera day, and stood on our servants' shoulders to see the *jatiya* (buffalo) being sacrificed,' Mother said. Dussera or Vijaya Dashami, the day the Goddess slew the buffalo demon, is also my mother's birthday. She had been named Gaura—the fair one—after the Goddess. She had, however, taken on another pen-name as a writer. Shivani, she called herself, the beloved of Shiva. 'After the ceremony, the priest put a blood *tika* (mark) on our foreheads and blessed us,' Mother said. She also told us how when a son was born, a goat was sacrificed at God Golu's temple and the meat was cooked within the temple premises on woodfire and distributed as holy *prasad* to all the members of the clan. 'It tasted good, you know,' mother added ruminatingly.

She was married into a Vaishnavite family later, and turned a vegetarian perforce. She could not eat the meat offerings from her mother's house anymore, for as a married woman she had changed her girlhood Gods for her husband's. The Goddesses, however, remained with her. They belong to no side in particular, and come when you call out to them, she said, as she picked up her pen to write.

♎ ♎ ♎

'Your mother changes completely when she sits down to write,' Father used to say with a mirthless laugh. He should have known.

The Tale of Nanda-Sunanda

For the women of the Himalayan region of Uttarakhand, the source of their fierce unbending pride is that the mother of all proud women—Sati—was reborn as Parvati and then re-reborn as Nanda Devi, in the royal family of Chand that ruled in the region. Nanda was followed by her sister Sunanda, and together became patron Goddesses of the whole area.

In a terrain where women daily carry headloads that would fell an ox in the plains, the two royal sisters refused to be regal exceptions to the local work-ethic. One day, while they were foraging for fuel and fodder in the forests that flanked the steep slopes of the hills, a demon, disguised as a water-buffalo, is said to have charged them. The sisters ran madly for cover with the demon in hot pursuit. Tree after tree refused them shelter for fear of incurring the demon's wrath. Cover was finally granted them by the lowly and soft Kadali, the banana tree. The demon was duly slain and the sisters went on to become the chief Goddesses for the region, with the twin peaks of the Himalayas named after them and dubbed as their permanent abodes. Each year, during the Sharadiya Navratri festival, men and women of the Uttarakhand area sing and dance for nine days before the images of Nanda and Sunanda, carved out of banana tree trunks. And then the sisters depart for their heavenly abode in a palanquin, seen off by the scions of the royal Chands.

There were many stories about the temples to other divine manifestations of Parvati: Bhramari Devi, Shyama Devi, Shitala Devi, Tripura-Sundari Devi. Then there were their wild female followers, the *Yoginis*, or demi-goddesses on earth, whose tiny white tombstones dotted various orchards in and around the town. (The *Yoginis* and their male counterparts, the *Siddhas*, were not cremated but interred after death.)

Mother told us how one of her naughty cousins had urinated on one of the memorials, upon being dared to do so by other children, and had been seriously ill immediately after for a long, long time.

'Those that dared him were beaten black and blue with stinging nettle whips, but what did we know? We were children,' Mother smiled.

Another aunt capped this with the story about the *Lati Yogini* (the mute one). She was the one who had chopped off her tongue as a sacrifice to Kali. 'Not a thread of clothing did she have on her, not a thread, remember? And how she pulled on the hashish in her clay pipe and made the flame leap up three spans high, like a man. She slept near the embers from dying pyres in the Someshwar cremation grounds, totally unafraid of the terrible ghosts and demons that lurked there. In fact, some said they heard her converse and laugh with unseen companions. Only men would dare go see her, only men!' the aunt said and the women rolled their eyes like mad cows.

What has suddenly made religion so humourless and tense in our time? When did the Goddess' devotees begin to recite her charms to the people in a way that strained out all laughter and wit? Even genuine doubt is getting rare.

The Tale of Aunt Nandi

When she was eighteen, we were told, Nandi, one of our great-aunts, also named after the Goddess, had hair so long that she had to stand upon the staircase to wash it. On a nice sunny day, we were told, it'd take her a whole day to dry it. This Aunt Nandi we never saw. She had died young of a broken heart, when her young husband disappeared with a band of wandering sadhus, Grandmother said. The husband did return shortly before World War Two, by which time his broken-hearted wife was already dying. She just turned her face to the wall when he entered the room and refused to speak or even look at him, Grandmother said, 'She died without saying anything, without perhaps forgiving anyone. Actually, only Goddesses may have beauty and lustrous hair and still evade bad luck. For us women, it is luckier to be plain and humble,' she said, sighed, and rolled her eyes.

I went to Grandmother as a young bride with my once long hair freshly bobbed and styled in my first trip to a beauty salon in New Delhi. She shook her head in disapproval, 'Your mother-in-law is too lenient with you. Does a bride allow a barber's scissors ever to touch her tresses? No! I do not like this.'

I pointed out humbly that my head felt much lighter and that I was also rid of having to comb, wash and braid those wild tresses. 'My husband likes it better, too, you know,' I added with the authority of a young wife.

'But your father and father-in-law are not going to like it' Grandmother said darkly. But before she said this she looked around to make sure that there were no older men present. 'I know men,' she added and rolled her eyes exactly like her daughters.

Ω   Ω   Ω

All the women I knew gave voice to unutterable thoughts when men were not around and women were discussing themselves and the Goddess, in that order. Brahmin priests were some of the few males allowed within the family precincts, for rituals. They were party to the talk, of course, for they carried almanacs, horoscopes of marriageable boys and girls and juicy tidbits of gossip about other families in the town: about how so-and-so's daughter had a flawed Mars and the family were looking for a boy in whose horoscope Mars was in a similarly questionable position, but that, of course, they were keeping all this under wraps. About how so-and-so had been making sly enquiries at the local Arya Samaj temple about conversion of a non-Hindu into a Hindu. 'Hmm . . . wasn't their son studying in the "land of the Angrez?" ' one of the women would ask, and nudge the others, 'does that mean a white daughter-in-law?'

'Oh my mother,' someone would exclaim, 'and in the house of one who got his cooking fuel washed in holy Ganges water? May the Goddess help them!'

How the women giggled behind their veils.

Of course no one would laugh out loud. Fathers and fathers-in-law would not like it. It would be tempting Fate.

How Aunt Paru Quelled the In-Laws

When Paru, one of my aunts, was a young bride, one of her brothers brought her a cashmere cardigan from England. She must have boasted about it often among the women in the family, as they sat cleaning grains, washing clothes or knitting in the sun. So one day at mealtime her mother-in-law, a sharp-tongued matriarch, remarked in acid tones to no one in particular, how one of the daughters-in-law in the family was going all English-English, and may one day solicit the English Queen's only daughter's hand in marriage for her son.

'I said nothing then,' Aunt Paru said, 'because as a daughter-in-law you are not supposed to have a tongue in your head in your father-in-law's house. But after that, throughout the entire winter months in the hills, I wore no woollens. People urged and urged me, but I'd just look at my husband's mother, and say no. When I nearly died of pneumonia, my mother-in-law finally broke down and wept and apologised and said, may the tiger take her tongue if she had meant ill.'

♎   ♎   ♎

Possibly this tale was meant by our virtuous aunt to illustrate both her steadfast loyalty to her natal family and also her personal pride. We, as young marriageable girls, were to understand from this how shrewish mothers-in-law may be brought to their knees by passive resistance, the terrible power of self-negation and how you must punish yourself to punish others.

It may even have been a daughter's commentary on her devotion to her family, though, knowing my Aunt Paru, this did not seem too likely.

But that is lore for you. Open-ended, like the story about Aunt Paru's cardigan from England.

More Tales of the Goddess

⬥

1995: A story about Nanda Devi is being told often in the central Himalayan region these days. The year was 1818, and the town was Almora. The British divisional commissioner Traille Sahib ordered the temple of the Devi relocated to make room for his revenue offices near the king's palace.

The locals tried talking to him, not angrily, for that would not do with a white man, but persistently. Nothing availed of it. Ill at ease, they watched him go on a trek to the Himalayan ranges, and feelings of impending doom persisted. They were confirmed when word came from the inner mountains that Traille Sahib had been blinded in a snow storm while trekking to the peak of Nanda Devi; the abode of the Goddess. The blindness, the doctors said, was caused by the glare of the snow, but the locals continued to trace it to the wrath of the Goddess. Traille Sahib was persuaded to take back his orders for moving the temple and to perform a puja. His eyesight returned, as suddenly as it had gone, once this was done.

A small story of Devi's worshippers for Devi's

worshippers by Devi's worshippers. Those who are not, may make what they can of it.

♎ ♎ ♎

Raw truth, like virgin snow, blinds. Unless you are used to it.

'Never show the storeroom to men,' grandmothers in this region say often. 'Since they do not do the cooking, they are not used to seeing foodstuff in the raw, and the sight confuses them into thinking there is more food in the house than there really is.' Men are squanderers, goes an ancient warning. Food, to them is something to be quickly swallowed. Their only excitement lies in warfare. They do not know that if women were not there to preserve their seed, they would cease to be.

It's true women themselves do not like warfare. But when they do pick up weapons, they too become warriors.

Like Kali. She knows war.

If she retreats it is only to return.

The Dark Temptress

Another story from the *Markandeya Purana*. Brothers Shumbh and Nishumb, two demons who have been terrorising the three worlds, are suddenly smitten with lust. It has so happened that their courtiers have seen the fair goddess Parvati bathing in a mountain river and have rushed home to tell their lascivious masters that their royal treasures will be incomplete till they add this jewel to them. In the manner of the powerful, Shumbh and Nishumb order that she be brought to them by force.

The messengers rush back to the Goddess.

Upon being propositioned by Shumbh and Nishumbh's messengers, the Goddess smiles and challenges them to a duel. The messengers are aghast.

'Do not give way to such pride, O Goddess,' one says, 'when even the Gods cannot beat my masters, how can you, a woman, hope to face their joint powers? Listen to me. Know your limitations and agree to come along, or else they may drag you there by your hair.'

'You are right,' giggles the Goddess, all feminine vulnerability, 'but silly me, I had taken this stupid vow that I would sleep only with the man who defeated me in battle.' 'But,' she adds coyly, 'please tell them this most respectfully, and let them then decide.'

The brothers Shumbh and Nishumbh are strangely excited by the request. They send an army headed by Dhoomralochan—he of the smouldering eyes. The lusty general is instructed to kill any man or God who tries to protect this arrogant female, and then drag her by her hair to the demons' abode. The army moves in serpentine lines, to humiliate the proud woman.

The brothers wait, salivating.

Ω   Ω   Ω

1995: Girls are being dragged in to brothels from far-flung districts like Vijaywada, Chilakaluri Peta, Nizamabad, Kakinada, Husnabad and many others. One girl, trying to escape, is caught by the touts who disfigure her face by pouring acid on it. An army of goons with bristling moustaches guards the brothels day and night. To escape the police, a new system of 'roving prostitution' has been invented. *Udayan,* a major Telugu daily, reports that this demon-army of brothel-keepers and their touts has amassed wealth beyond belief. This is used to entice fresh entrants to the trade.

Teenage prostitution has been flourishing in this southern Deccan plateau town of Yadagiri Gatta. According to unofficial estimates there are forty-four brothels here. All these are flourishing, notwithstanding protests by local women, because everyone except the women wants them to flourish: the police, the politicians, the local administration.

The younger and more aggressive the prostitute, the higher the demand.

If women are being sold, can liquor be far behind? Locally brewed arrack runs like water. Men and boys stagger about as their hapless wives and hungry children cry themselves hoarse.

☊   ☊   ☊

The first rumblings of the Goddess are heard. Women have stopped being nice. They begin to overturn the jeeps of the dealers and chase the police out with sticks. They will not let the killer brew enter their villages. Men hit them, tear their clothes, some are even dragged in the dirt, but they continue to picket the arrack shops.

The prostitutes applaud and join up. They too have children. And they hate the furtive alcoholics.

Elections are round the corner. The leader of the Opposition is wily Nandmuri Taraka Rama Rao, a man well known for playing God on the Telugu silver screen. He hears of these women and realizes the golden opportunity. If he is returned to power, he thunders from his election vehicle camouflaged to look like a traditional *ratham*, he shall cancel the licences of all breweries and liquor dealers. It is rumoured that at night he sleeps in a sari with earrings in his earlobes because an astrologer has predicted a woman-like creature shall rule the Deccan.

He knows about woman-power.

He wins the election, largely assisted by women voting for him as a bloc.

♎   ♎   ♎

The Goddess merely grunts when the mightly general Dhoomralochan petitions her on behalf of his lord. The grunt decimates him, smouldering eyes and all, before he has completed his speech.

Then the Goddess and her lion go gleefully on a rampage, mauling the demon army. As the demons flee, screaming curses and threatening revenge, the Goddess laughs.

Another army is sent, accompanied this time by two mighty generals Chanda and Munda, instructed once again to drag the obstinate woman back, by her hair.

This time the Goddess grows really angry. And from her arises the most fearsome Kali, in a tiger-skin and wearing a garland of skulls and bones. Her face is wrinkled and fierce; her eyes, glow like two balls of fire.

Kali shakes her wild mane and enters the fearful ranks of demons, flourishing a cleaver. Some demons she chops to bits, others, together with elephants with huge bells around their necks, she swallows whole, brass bells and all.

♎   ♎   ♎

1995: The world is being globalised. A few months have passed after Rama Rao's ban on liquor. The powerful liquor lobby petitions the state High Court. It is our democratic right to earn a livelihood, they say. The Court agrees.

The women look to N.T. Rama Rao. The chief minister maintains a diplomatic silence, very much in vogue among politicians, from Delhi in the north to Andhra in the south. Then he leaves for London, to invite foreign investment from British industry and rich non-resident Indians in the West, into his state. The women are forgotten. Men from the secretariat in Hyderabad hold talks with men who own distilleries, regardless of the women.

The rumble rises again. The walls of the secretariat begin to shake. Women point their fingers and remind all that care to listen that the Parliamentary elections are only a few months away. Do the members of Parliament wish to get the women's vote again? Yes? Then please contact your man in London, and get him to cancel the court order.

Faxes begin to fly like arrows. Finally they penetrate the ring of security and reach the Chief Minister as he sits confabulating about foreign capital investments.

At midnight Rama Rao's message arrives. The liquor licences are not to be renewed, and the state government shall petition the Supreme Court of India against the verdict. The wary bureaucracy sets out to compy with the orders. The liquor lobby hurls curses.

Women have won. But just about.

The liquor lobby retires, hurt, cross and full of evil plans about how it will tap the market in adjacent states and how once these elections are over, things will change.

The women smile. Theirs is not an innocent smile either.

They know the obstinacy of the colour black. Haven't they washed the dirty linen of the world?

♎   ♎′   ♎

When the generals Chanda and Munda advance towards her, wild with lust and fury, Kali laughs. She laughs a most cruel, fearsome laugh and her bloody canines gleam. 'Humm,' she growls, and catching Chanda by his hair, separates his head from his body with one blow.

Likewise Munda.

Bouncing the two severed heads in her hands like two balls, Kali giggles and presents them playfully to her friend, the Goddess Chandika, as war-trophies and as good-luck charms for her future battles.

'Dear sister, thank you,' says the fearsome Chandika, 'from now on you will also be known as Chamunda, the bouncer of severed heads.' The Goddesses laugh as together they play with the blood-dripping orbs.

As predicted by Kali, Shumbh and Nishumbh materialize on the scene with their myriad armies. By now Chandi too enjoying herself and is permitted to lead the attack. When she sees the brothers advance, she twangs her bow playfully and another fearsome group of female warriors emerges from her body. Then some more emerge from the bodies of all the male Gods in the pantheon, who are cowering on the fringes of the battlefield, unable to face the demons. Thus do the nine Shaktis arrive. Chamunda riding a ghost, Laxmi upon a floating lotus, Brahmi riding a swan, Maheshwari upon the back of a bull, Kaumari on a peacock, Vaishnavi, sitting astride on a Garuda bird, Varahi on a boar, Ishwari in white robes sitting astride a bull and Indrani on an elephant. All of them armed to the teeth, and raring to fight. Together they take over the field.

♎   ♎   ♎

The nine Shaktis produce a wild ululation, like millions of she-jackals baying in a dark forest, as the Goddess winks at them. Then, with a straight face, she says to them that she will give the demons another chance. She is willing to withold her hand, to prevent a carnage. So she has asked her husband Shiva, he with the long matted tresses, to go and tell the demons that if they care for their lives, they should rush back to the netherworld they inhabit. Should they choose to face the Goddess and her fierce female companions, they shall be chewed up and swallowed.

The Goddesses ululate.

The demons are appalled when Shiva delivers this message from the female warriors. They are sure he is jesting. They are furious and rush towards the female army, flourishing their weapons, and gnashing their teeth.

The Goddess twangs her bow again, and then shoots off a volley of arrows that knocks down the demons' first line of defence completely.

She had warned them, hadn't she?

Then her companions swing into action.

While the lesser demons are being taken care of,

a fierce demon called Raktabeej—he whose drops of blood form seeds for the instant birth of similar demons—rushes up, flourishing his mace. Each arrow that pierces him and draws blood, produces millions of demons that spread out all over the battlefield. The Gods, who are mere onlookers, blanch. This promises to be a tricky situation. Surely the Shaktis would be powerless to tackle this demonic phenomenon.

But the Goddess laughs. She loves war and she loves challenges. As Chandi, she casts an amused glance at the crestfallen faces of the Gods and then calls up her sister Chamunda. She asks her to drink up the demon's blood before even a drop of it falls to the ground and gets transformed into more and more demons. And when Raktabeej hits out at Chandi next, she shoots a volley of arrows, and fearsome Chamunda, as Kali, her bloodshot eyes rolling in drunken ecstasy, begins to lap up his blood.

The Gods look away.

The demon collapses and dies. The remaining demons flee.

The Goddess ululates. The battle is won.

The powers and the Goddess now break into a dance of victory, drunk with blood and success. This is no ordinary warrior, the brothers Shumbh and Nishumbh realize. They gird their loins to come face to face with the woman. They are strangely excited.

♎   ♎   ♎

With a cry that could kill children in the womb, the enemies stand face to face.

There is a moment of tense silence. Then the Goddess blows on her conchshell, twangs her bow, sets her bells ringing and all her elephants and lions begin to trumpet and roar on cue.

In the melee that follows, all the demons including Nishumb are slain, and the female warriors, along with the Goddess, devour and drink and carry on the grisly slaughtering with undisguised glee.

Nishumbh is dead.

Only Shumbh is left now. He, in the manner of all bad losers, first chooses to heckle the goddess, 'You do not know that your show of prowess with such anger fools no one. You coward! Like all women you seek shelter behind other women and fight unfairly with their help. Let me see what you are worth alone.'

Once again, silence descends. Slowly, one by one, all the powers of the Goddess disappear into her.

Once again the Goddess stands, alone and supreme.

'All these, you fool,' says the Goddess, 'were my own manifestations. Come forward, I shall take you on alone.'

They begin to fight. First they fight with weapons on the ground. Then, as he stands defeated on the earth, Shumbh suddenly pounces on the Goddess and carries her into the skies.

Up there they begin to wrestle unarmed.

With a bellow, the Goddess finally picks up the demon and hurls him down towards the earth, and when the demon tries to rush back, she kills him with one sharp jab of her spear, the *shoola*.

The end of Shumbh.

The battle too is over. The possibilities of future ones are not over, though. Black looms forever on the horizon. This, only the Goddess knows.

So as she goes back to her abode in the snow-capped mountains of the north, the Goddess assures the Gods that she shall be born and reborn each time the demons arise and they are threatened.

'I shall be born as Shakti in the house of Yashoda, the wife of Nand.'

'I shall be born as Raktdantika (she with the blood-stained teeth) to kill the demon Vaiprachitta.'

'I shall be born at the end of the hundred-year drought as Shatakshi—she of the hundred eyes.'

'I shall be born variously as Shakambhari, the Goddess of plants; as Durga, the killer of the demon Durgam, as Bhima, the killer of the band of demons that torture saints, and as Bhramari, the queen bee, she of the six legs, who shall be the killer of the demon Arun.'

☊   ☊   ☊

'Yes, yes, but for the time being go home, Mother,' urge the Gods, keen to resume their normal lives. They do not know why the dark, violent and fearless Kali still lingers, uncontrollable and unmatched. Her drunken eyes roll, her gait wobbles, she opens her mouth to utter a wild ululation from time to time.

'Go home, Mother,' the Gods beseech, 'thank you for destroying the forces of darkness. Please rest now.'

Of all the manifestations of the warrior Goddess, the one hardest to cope with is the one after battle. A wild and disorderly storm continues to grow and grow within the Goddess like a cancerous gene that has forgotten how to stop mutating. At this point the Goddess may even incite those close to her to a mad frenzy of destruction. The Gods pray to her again and again: 'Go, Mother, go.'

According to a tale, during the period of near madness that followed the slayings of the demons Shumbha and Nishumbha, the Goddess urged her male consort Shiva to join her in a wild dance in which she matched him pirouette to pirouette, gesture to gesture. Only when he raised one leg to the skies did she remember her feminity, and overcome by embarrassment, slowly calmed down and became normal.

Another, parallel, tale begs to differ. According to it, the Goddess continued to dance even after her companion collapsed. As her madness grew, Shiva called out to her like a frightened child and slowly the mad dance came to a halt.

♎   ♎   ♎

One after another, like both the dark and benign Goddesses the Goddess carries within her, the stories with different endings move on.

The Tale of Badi Amma

Towards the end of her days, our Badi Amma was a woman who raged and raged against her dwindling life. In her heyday, when our uncle was alive, she had been a most loving, giving, though somewhat domineering and powerful person. Upon her husband's death, she had willingly let go of the reins of control over her family and retired to a small house in the hills. But that did not prove to be the end of her story. Once she let go of power, she craved for control all over again. It was then that sooty-black rages began to envelope her.

The sons brought her back to live with them.

But Badi Amma, we were told by the daughters-in-law tearfully, was hell to live with when she descended from the hills. As a widowed woman, living with her sons, she began feeling like a guest in the house. She became restless and accusatory and miserable. If the family's entire day was not planned around her, she sulked. Nothing pleased her. If people didn't visit her, she'd complain; if they did, she'd say it tired her.

As her nieces, we listened to her complaints and we suffered with her but we also grew ashamed of her frequent and peurile displays of foot-stamping petulance. We would make offers that were rudely, almost curtly refused, and gradually we felt our daughterly sympathies drain away. Our poor cousins-in-law had it tough, we agreed.

Would she like to go visiting her relatives, her sons suggested. Badi Amma was furious.

What? Sit with those silly chattering oldies with their rattling dentures and festering fistulas, who did not know their backsides from the moon?

'Out of the question,' the sons said they had been told.

All right. Would she like to go abroad to visit her own siblings then? Go to the USA on a tourist visa perhaps, we suggested gingerly.

No, she'd read enough to know there was nothing for old people there. They just sat in long hopeful rows in parks, like crows at a *shraddha* ceremony and stared and stared. She didn't wish to die of boredom in an alien land and return home in an urn, she said.

No, let her go back to the hills, she said. No matter how snowed-under the house, how bad the servants, she'd not like to be a burden. She had eyes in her head, she said.

Silence grew. Also tension.

Like a brilliant general after a war, the suddenly dispensable warrior-mother was relentlessly using her fury and her grief like a *Sudershan chakra* upon us. She marred conjugal happiness wherever she saw it. Everything about the young angered her:

their laughter, their horseplay, a wife's whispered asides to her husband or a half-seen caress.

'You have lost your *samskaras* and society its moorings,' she said.

She raged and she drove people away. Then she complained about how the young had become ungrateful and unloving.

What do we do then, the men and women in her family asked each other. The family had no answers.

♎   ♎   ♎

Death arrived in spring after months of slow and smelly depletion. It was a dark moonless night filled with the hard noise of laboured breathing that halted with one last shiver. After that, only the relentless whine of the mosquitoes.

Today as I sit and unravel this legendary aunt's life, I wonder.

When was Badi Amma last herself? Before she lost one breast and then another, before the spine gave way and bent that proud Brahmin frame double, before her body shrank and shrank into a pathetic mummy of leather and bone, before she began gulping at air and still falling short of a whole breath, before those once bright eyes clouded over with milky cataracts so she could no longer sit squinting at TV close-ups of crowds attending rallies, to find out if her elder son was there?

When did Badi Amma decide to leave the battlefield? Was it when she heard us begging her to stay, secretly hoping that she'd leave? Did she know then, that like Kali, she had overstayed and decided to take revenge?

You cannot deceive the Goddess. She'll move when she wants to, not when you do. If you are suspiciously polite, too obsequious, she is going to be very angry indeed.

Ω   Ω   Ω

And when she has moved on you will discover a great big black hole that nothing but nothing shall fill.

This is when you wish and do not wish. You hope yet do not hope.

This is when you begin to write.

Saraswati

'Why do the river waters make a sound like a woman weeping?' the mighty king Vikramaditya is once said to have asked his court poet Kalidasa.

'Whyever not?' retorted the poet. 'If you were a girl born in the faraway mountains, and were then married off to a saline sea far away, never to return to your father's house, would you also not weep and weep?'

♎   ♎   ♎

Saraswati forms the earliest example of a Goddess who derives her name from a river. Or was it that the river was named after her?

'Never name a girl after a river,' one of our grand-aunts remarked darkly once. 'A girl that bears the name of a river shall always be estranged from her father and her natal family. Remember your aunt Ganga?'

♎   ♎   ♎

Rivers such as the Ganges and Yamuna have long been worshipped in India as Goddesses. The triad of the three great northern rivers, Ganga, Yamuna and Saraswati, is also associated with the three great ones. Ganga is associated with Shiva, Yamuna with Vishnu (through his incarnation as Krishna) and Saraswati with Brahma. Perhaps in the first stage of her evolution as a deity, Saraswati was a water deity, being an important and sacred river with somewhat saline water (the word *saras* also means salt). In the next stage, Saraswati gets identified with the varied rituals performed on her banks. This fact also links her with the composition of hymns and with two cerebral demi-goddesses, Ida and Bharati. During the Puranic age as Vac Devi (the Goddess of the spoken word), the concept of Saraswati was further meshed with the concept of the Goddess as Gayatri, that most famous and sacred of all Brahmanical *mantras*, and personified later as the second wife of Prajapati, or Brahma, the creator.

Not a home-lover like Laxmi, the Goddess of plenty, Saraswati chooses vast open spaces to wander in dreamily, drifting from place to place. Time can be no threat to her since as Vac, or language, she herself is a repository of time, and can restructure it at will. Space poses her no boundaries and unlike the warrior Kali, she has no need for companions in power either. Brimful of peace, Saraswati is like the gentle rain over the seas.

The Tale of the Aunt and the Goddess with River-Names

We did not know, initially, that at birth our aunt Badi Amma was named Ganga, after the mighty river. She underwent several changes of name later, but her mother, to her dying day, called her Ganga.

The reason why the same aunt got to be better

known first as Lalita and then as Badi Amma or the 'big mother,' was that once she learnt of the superstition about river names, she insisted that her name be changed to Lalita, or the Goddess of many forms. So Lalita it was. This was the name with which she was admitted to primary school. Eventually, however, she got to be known neither as Ganga nor as Lalita, but as Badi Amma. The reason being that everything about her was big. A big round face, a big mouth, big eyes, and a big red dot on her high forehead. But biggest of all were her breasts, which jutted out of that huge frame like two enormous sliding domes.

Her mother said, as a baby, Lalita nee Ganga had been surprisingly puny and frail, being premature. But she survived, first because girls are survivors no matter how unwanted; and secondly because an exceptionally powerful conjunction of stars guarded her birth. On the twelfth day after her birth, she was named Ganga. As she lay in her mother's lap, the family priest said her name in her ear through a conch shell, thrice: Ganga, Ganga, Ganga. Her birth star was the tenacious Capricorn or Makara, and the Sun in her horoscope was in an elevated position. She was thus destined to be proud, obstinate and ambitious. And also a leader.

♎   ♎   ♎

In myth and lore, the story of Saraswati runs somewhat like this. Out of the mind of Prajapati Brahma, the great bearded father of mankind, a winsome beauty Saraswati, was born. But once he saw her, the Creator fell in love with his creation and wanted to mate with her. The *Manas Putri* (mind-daughter) fled the grasp of this lusty old father-turned-predator. But Brahma was not one to give up. He pursued her first in one direction, then in another. To keep a closer vigil on his mercurial offspring, he also began to grow one head after another upon his shoulders and ended up with five. But Saraswati still eluded him.

Brahma was angry. He, being the Creator, was also all powerful, in the manner of all fathers. We do not know how, but Badi Amma told us that legend has it that he did manage to marry the elusive girl, and produced through her mind the four great *Vedas*. Lore also has it that Brahma discovered that his girl-wife was too aloof and absent-minded for his liking. He had arranged for a major fire-sacrifice, at which his wife's appearance by his side was a must. He repeatedly warned Saraswati not to take too long over her toilet and miss the auspicious hour. She must, he had decreed, take her traditional seat to his left, well in time. But Saraswati behaved with her characteristic whimsical disregard for parental diktats. Her prolonged toilet saw to it that the holy hour passed without the couple's making the supreme joint offering to the fire God as man and wife. When Saraswati finally arrived, Brahma was livid. He threw her out, and replaced her with the daughter of a sage, called Gayatri.

Another parallel lore says, however, that when that celestial busybody, saint Narada, once happened to go where Brahma and Saraswati sat, he sang Saraswati's praises so loud and long that Brahma grew jealous and threw her out.

Anyway, according to all the stories, a furious Saraswati is said to have been thrown out by her husband. It is said that before leaving, she cursed Brahma that he'd be worshipped no more than once a year. The curse still holds.

In spite of, or perhaps because of, this curse, Saraswati was offered as a gift by Brahma to his grandson-in-law and friend Shiva, as a wife or a helper. Shiva and Brahma were later to become fierce enemies because Shiva's dear wife Sati, was driven to suicide by Brahma's son Daksha. Whether she was palmed off to Shiva as a wife or a surrogate daughter, by ex-husband Brahma, Saraswati's relationship with Shiva was not too happy either. After Sati's suicide, Shiva, in a fit of fury is said to have lopped off one of the five heads of Brahma and also disfigured his daughter Saraswati's nose. He raged against them because both were present at the site but had failed to prevent the tragedy.

$$\Omega \qquad \Omega \qquad \Omega$$

Think about it.

Saraswati sits at the site of Daksha's fire sacrifice, unwanted and uncaring. It is as if she can see Sati's end already.

Her presence is that of a woman unwanted by father and husband. She is an embarrassing reminder of their secret practices and their hidden desires. Her silence, precarious and ambiguous as it is, speaks louder than words.

Thus are Goddesses with river-names.

Badi Amma Turns Seventeen

To continue our story about Badi Amma, the aunt with a river-name, there was the time when Ganga, now referred to as Lalita, was seventeen and wanted to be a writer and a scholar. By then her father was in faraway England and her grandfather was eighty and almost sightless. Mornings he summoned her, his favourite grandchild, and let her read to him, in sonorous tones, Sanskrit poems full of an ageless wisdom and grief.

She would read a few couplets. Grandfather would be silent. Thinking him to be asleep, she would stop. But he would say 'Continue'.

And she would.

The only variation to this routine would be the writing of the letters on Grandfather's behalf to his son, her father, who had almost broken away from the conservative family and settled in England. Lalita would prod Grandfather for the closing lines so she could finish the letter. The old man would sit silent for a long while, then say, 'There's nothing more to write, except to say, do not marry a white woman now, to deepen my shame. I'd rather you stayed away when I die. But one day, when your own children cause you grief like you've to me, you'll remember my words.'

As he said this through her to his son, his rheumy blind eyes, like dull cowrie shells, would be full of unshed tears. Lalita would wince and glance out of the window.

On one such occasion, Lalita's mother called her children inside to a fresh, hot meal. Her brothers were home from public school hostels run by Jesuit priests, where they were forced to eat lukewarm puddings and gristly stews all through the term. They were the first to reach the kitchen. The choicest bits of food and the best seats were always theirs for the asking. The sisters were expected to squeeze in anywhere.

Lalita delayed entering the kitchen as long as she could and was always the first to come out. She sat for a long time among the cool shaded spots near the *sun jai* creepers, trying to gather her thoughts. How can you know what you miss, if you've never seen it? In the dappled silence of the courtyard, there were no answers, only a dripping tap and the slow soft clap of a loose tin sheet on the roof.

Somewhere along the line, Lalita had begun learning Sanskrit from her grandfather.

Grandfather abhorred English, the language of the white *mlechhas*, whose land had lured away his beloved son, forever. He also despised all those who studied it in public schools and thought they would thus become sahibs. With an enormous heave he shed his misgivings about teaching *Devbhasha*—the language of the Gods—to a girl, for she alone among his grandchildren had resisted English. Lalita to him became the reason to live, to talk. Sitting cross-legged on the floor, he even taught her the secret invocation to the sun God—the *Gayatri Mantra*—which men for seven generations past had whispered only in the ears of their sons so women and lower castes would not hear it.

That summer became unforgettable for Lalita. As she began to learn the lusty love poetry of Amaru, of Kalidasa, and Bhartrihari, smells and colours startled her young blood into wanting too much, to remember forgotten wishes. To touch and to gaze and gaze and to touch. But she had to slow down to learn the hymn to the young sun, Savita, the giver of wisdom and insight.

As the pale sun poured into the room, Lalita found thoughts of the young princess Kunti, of the *Mahabharata*, she who was seduced and impregnated by the Sun, crossing and recrossing her invocation. Slowly, as she recited the powerful *mantra*, the room filled with passion and moist dreams. Boy cousins seemed to look strangely at girl cousins, and bumble bees got drunk on nectar and buzzed round and round. A great entangled forest of many passions began to grow around her with huge fleshy flowers that gleamed and gleamed and beckoned with immense lips. Come, they said. Come. Come.

The short, hard and masculine chant assailed her senses. Only when it was over did all the pungent daily details return; the smells from her mother's kitchen, the sudden laughter and screams of children, the attar-laced tobacco fumes from a silver hookah, the amber pine-resin drops upon floors freshly polished with cow-dung. Slowly, the sensual jungle began to fade.

Knowledge alone endured, hard and magnificient like the sun itself.

Lalita learnt with constancy. How to handle those intricate and ancient verbal combinations, the substantive and the adjectival, how to survive in the midst of an ancient masculine learning, alone and impregnable.

No woman in the family had done this before her.

Even with his blind eyes the grandfather could make out a great mind flexing and stretching, even rearing at him with a newly unfolding power. 'Continue,' he said simply, when she paused. 'Continue.'

And she did.

Of the missing son, Grandfather never talked. But once every few months, when he made Lalita write him the letter, he made sure to give him the dates for all the auspicious and inauspicious days to come. There were dates for changing the sacred thread and the date for his mother's memorial *shraddha*. He knew the son would not be bothered with observing any of these. But these were the motions that had to be gone through, for hurting with love, for revenge. It was an elaborate game the old man went on playing with his son through his rebellious granddaughter, she of the sign of the devious Capricorn. She, he knew, loved and hated her father as he loved and hated his son. She watched and listened to him closely, wonderingly. Like him, she too could yank open sealed doors to pain and memory, and face the risk like a true Brahmin without flinching.

When she hesitated, he simply said, 'Continue'.

Sanskrit, a resistance to English and the missing father. These were the links that attached Lalita to her blind grandfather like an umbilical cord. But both were too proud, too cunning to break the silence or acknowledge the other. In silence, when they felt the pulse of love, they smiled to themselves.

In silence, Lalita learned never to forget or trust the other completely.

Ω   Ω   Ω

Gayatri, Savitri and Saraswati. The three are described variously as the three forms the Goddess of learning assumes in the morning, noon and evening. According to some legends she emerged out of the mouth of the dark god Krishna and in later Buddhist tales, Saraswati is associated with Manjushri, the Buddhist God of learning.

In Maharashtra, Saraswati is often portrayed as one of the two wives of the erudite elephant-headed God Ganesha, the son of Parvati. Of the two common links Saraswati and Ganesha have, one is a father who punishes and then gives the child the rare boon of true intelligence, the other is a pure love of learning.

It figures. As the commemorative power Vac, once maligned, Saraswati chooses to enter neither the home nor the hearth, but goes off to loiter pensively along the lonely banks of river or in the forests all by herself. She thus creates an unshakeable individual identity and a history that later lore about her sisters may seek to destroy or erase but cannot. She is memory, pitted implacably against power, and all the verbal ruses power has spawned to gain control over minds.

Mulling over Saraswati, one realizes that all her children must at some point or another pose unanswerable questions to themselves through their chosen craft. Also recognize that those who share the creative qualities of the mind with Saraswati, are mostly destined to be like her: disinherited and exiled. But it is these exiles with no inheritance who have clung to history and felt the need to redeem it from oblivion at all costs. What makes the effort somewhat worthwhile is the fact that at times of stress, all of them come to share something of Saraswati's composure, her curious calm and a certain brackish humour that coexists with equal degrees of sorrow and compassion.

$$\Omega \quad \Omega \quad \Omega$$

The poet Mahadevi Verma, when I first met her, was already an ageing woman. She was dressed in a simple white khadi sari with a long-sleeved blouse. Her voice was deep, almost like a man's. Her gaze made one pause. Here was someone who would not suffer fools gladly. People cleared their throats unconsciously when they spoke to her.

Mahadevi was telling my recently widowed mother, her fellow writer, about how she too had once decided to renounce the world and become a Hindu nun, in a *mutt*. What eventually changed her mind, she said, was an encounter with the head guru of the order she had wanted to join. 'When I entered the room, Shivani Ji,' she told my mother, 'would you believe, the old man covered his face with a palm-leaf fan. I was told it was because he had taken a vow never to look at a woman. At that I just left. What could I learn from a man who had so little trust in himself that he could not even look a woman in the eye?'

Men!

The two writers laughed long and loud.

Ω   Ω   Ω

In a photograph from those days, Badi Amma, my aunt Lalita, can be seen dressed in the odd, old-fashioned long skirt and long-sleeved blouse worn by the local peasant girls, with a languid arm resting above her head, and a strand of straggly hair hanging on her wide domed forehead. She was by then already beginning to be secretive and detached from the world of her mother and sisters. She had begun teaching, painting, writing and doing many things for her own secret reasons and not because they'd bring her money or approval. Women in the family were already in awe of her, the men were suspicious. Together they waited for her father to come back and straighten her out and marry her off to a man of their choice.

But instead the World War came, and soon after that, the Partition of the country, and then death.

Grandfather died soon after the war began in earnest, and for the twelve days that led to the feast on the thirteenth day of the mourning, Lalita would neither cry nor eat or speak. She sat in the corner where the old man used to sit, and read the holy *Gita* silently to his ghost: 'Just as the body sheds old clothes to take on new ones, so also the soul drops the old body to go and seek out a new one.'

Then she wrote a strange story called *The Red Brick House*. It was about a house partitioned along strange lines, drawn by hands, without eyes,

When this, her first story, was published in a prestigious journal, most people would not believe it had been written by one so young and a woman at that. Well-wishers asked her mother to get her married soon. The head of a delegation of visiting scholars who had read the story in translation, invited her to come and teach in the department of ancient languages in a far-away university. To all these Lalita said, no.

Running away was not something Lalita wanted to do. But she had also lost all desire to stay at home. Now she only wanted to do things which no one in her family would understand, so she'd never need their approval or feel guilty when the time came for her to move away. She walked around calmly, with her fury buried in sweet forgetfulness, waiting for her father to come and signal her release.

As her grandfather had predicted, his son came back soon after the old man's death.

Was her father glad? Or just guilt-ridden? Lalita was twenty-five then, and had learnt not to care either way. Her learning protected her like a tiger-skin. Lofty-browed and pitiless, she stood her ground in silence against the family. She wanted to go to a far-away college. Yes, yes, in the hot and rotting tropical plains of the east, where no woman from families like hers had ever set foot. She had already written to the college and had immediately been accepted.

Shall I go then? Her eyes asked her father as he looked up after reading the letter of acceptance.

The hopes in her eyes were proud, as once they were in his. He, who knew the limits by now, gave room.

That's the way life is, the melancholy son who had abandoned his own father, thought.

To her he simply said, 'Yes'.

And soon after that, Aunt Lalita left home.

The Children of
Saraswati

Neither Kali nor Laxmi were born. They just came to
be, perfect, fully grown and perfectly free. Of the
three great Goddesses, Saraswati is the only one
born with a known parent who fought for every bit of
her unique freedom. And the process of undoing her
chains guaranteed that she plumbed the depths of
those dark nether worlds of the mind which no
other Goddess had touched. Precocious girlhood,
parental abuse, broken marriage, Saraswati had
traversed them all. But confrontation or subterfuge
are not her style. Saraswati makes her peace with
all that has happened to her and around her, by first
rising above the heat of the moment through an
enormous heave of will, and then recollecting and
recording it in her memory meticulously. She is
detached because if she has to recreate experience,
she must rise above all family ties, loyalties, emotions
and passions.

Her colour is white, the colour of peace, of *Sattvas*.
Her clothes, the lotus she sits upon, and also her
familiar, the swan, are all white. Not for her Kali's
dramatic and gory nakedness, or Laxmi's dazzling

red and gold. Her robe and appearance show serenity
and a total lack of artifice.

Saraswati's ironical eye, one may be sure, watches
Kali's tussle for power against male demons and
Laxmi's subterfuges in the male world of power and
plenitude. But she remains a witness, a dispassionate
historian. She is one who believes in the ultimate
futility of all warfare and the trappings of wealth.

Understandably, such a Goddess could be
venerated by the simple-minded and earthy
householders, but not loved and fussed over by them
like her regal sister Laxmi, or even feared and held
in awe like Shakti. Saraswati remains the
unblemished ascetic goddess, to whom no temples
are built and who offers nothing except knowledge,
no institution, no protection, no riches.

$$\Omega \qquad \Omega \qquad \Omega$$

As early as the *Brahmana* anthologies, Saraswati
was referred to as Vac Devi—the goddess of speech.
Whenever a new baby arrives, grandmothers make a
five-pointed star—called Saraswati—sign on the
newborn's tongue with honey. The tongue, the organ
of speech, is thus expected to get hitched to
Saraswati's star early enough. The same star sign is
drawn on the wooden-framed slate—*pati*—when the
teacher introduces the child to the world of letters.

There was no statue of Saraswati in our family
puja room, but a picture wherein she sat upon a
swan: a white goddess with white garments who
played serenely upon her stringed *veena*. When we
were schoolchildren Saraswati was introduced to us
as Vidya Mata (mother of learning).

No special fasts or rituals were observed for her,

nor did she pop up in Grandmother's tales with the frequency of her sisters Laxmi and Parvati.

Ω Ω Ω

'No one shall die for me, as I shall die for none.'

Ω Ω Ω

Vakh is the name given to miscellaneous poems the mystic Kashmiri poetess, Laldyad (b. 1335), left behind. The term is derived, doubtless, from the word *vac*. It is said that this mystic poetess was born on the banks of the river Vitasta in a Brahmin farmer's house. Laldyad was married briefly to a pandit. Soon, they both realized that Laldyad was not cut out for marriage. But while the husband accepted this, the mother-in-law is said to have tortured the recalcitrant daughter-in-law incessantly. She could not understand why this strange daughter-in-law of hers lapsed into meditative silences instead of dressing up and socialising with friends and relatives. She starved Laldyad, made her do all the hard domestic chores and complained to the son incessantly. But nothing could bring Laldyad round.

One day, legend has it, Laldyad just dropped everything, including her garments, and wandered forth naked as a baby. She sang of her joys and her sorrows:

I did not carry a child, nor did I bring to birth.
Nor did I enjoy the sweets a new mother has.
Now I roam the world.

Laldyad left behind no monument . . .

'*No one shall die for me, nor will I die for anyone.*'

Strange acceptance this. Strange, the peace of Saraswati.

♎   ♎   ♎

All through our growing years, each time our feet touched a book, or even a torn piece of paper on which words in any langauge were printed, we were supposed to touch it to our foreheads and send up a prayer in apology to Saraswati, the mother of all learning. We worshipped her at the spring festival of Vasant Panchami with fresh spring flowers and berries. But even though she was of great interest to us as Vidya Mata, who helped us cram and pass exams, it intrigued me that she remained a Goddess of peripheral interest to our worldly mothers and grandmothers. I know now how, as women, they had recognised with their unerring instincts fairly early in life, that hitching their wagons to this brilliant white star and her cerebral, but chaste and celibate world was not really going to help them. Silences and meditations could hardly help them run a household, the only future open to them.

There really was nowhere to go, was there? Only lunatics shed clothes and inhibitions. Or female saints.

That way lay madness.

♎   ♎   ♎

As followers go, Kali's energetic devotees share the sensitivity of Saraswati's disciples, but not their cool and ironical detachment. Laxmi's followers, on the other hand, ignore the subtler shades of abstract experience, because they tend to focus mostly on gross products and worldly methods of production.

Followers of both Laxmi and Kali live in the immediacy of events they generate. Not so Saraswati's. Knowledge such as Saraswati's, by its very nature, co-exists with extreme sensitivity and suffering tempered with a magnificient tranquillity of soul. As Pashyanti, or perception, Saraswati generates the ability to grasp the finest shades of fleeting thought, as Madhyama, the capacity to ponder over them, and as Vac, the capacity to communicate it though with an ironical detachment from the experience itself.

As the disinherited daughter and estranged wife, Saraswati lives perpetually in self-imposed exile. She focuses her calm, dispassionate gaze upon the past as pure experience. Pratishruti, or the capacity to recall without anger or resentment, is Saraswati's greatest gift to her children: the writers, musicians and creators of various art forms. All of them have fought with tradition, but their fight has been cerebral, not emotional. For without cutting away the umbilical cord, no innovative new beginning may ever be made, whether one is creating or procreating. This is the message of Saraswati.

℧   ℧   ℧

Lore has it that on her birthday, just before she left home, our Aunt Lalita had dressed herself up as the celibate Goddess of learning. In a corroborative photograph her father took with his German camera, she can be seen dressed all in white. She is wearing a circle of wild flowers around her head, another round her neck and two smaller variations around her wrists. She is also playing on a stringed instrument and laughing in the eyes of her younger brother who has struck the pose of a humble devotee. Other siblings float around her in billowing dresses, like little swans.

♎ ♎ ♎

When aunt Lalita left, they say, she left with just a tin trunk that held some books and a bag of other essentials.

♎ ♎ ♎

There is another old snapshot of my aunt Lalita from those days, taken presumably on a late summer afternoon, in which she is shielding her eyes from the bright summer sun. The light is so bright that everyone looks coffee-coloured. Lalita's eyes are screwed up against the sun and her mouth is open. She's doubtless commanding the person taking the photograph. One hand is thrust out a little, either in warning or to hold down the flyaway *pallav* of her sari over her already ample breasts.

This was the year of her long vacation. This was when she came home from college and took to going for long walks all by herself.

This was the year the Japanese had crept closer to her country and begun bombing the hills in the east. When this began, her university was closed, and Lalita had to come home suddenly. During this year, she brought her great art teacher home. Between news of distant deaths and bombings, Lalita and the old man set out in our little hill town, to rediscover traditional natural dyes, handmade paper and Indian iconography.

Ω   Ω   Ω

Being rich and indulgent parents, Lalita's were not hit especially hard by the war-time scarcities. And living in the hills saved them from the communal riots raging in the plains of the north. They accepted the avuncular teacher with the great flowing white beard, who'd turned up with her just like that. Well, mother did grumble a bit initially, but then lost her resentment and smiled at him as she would at a respected sadhu visiting the family. She told him in mime—for she did not share his language—that she could serve him no meat or fish, all right? He mimed back to say that it was. After that peace reigned between the two.

It was also interesting for Lalita's father to watch the old painter observe and reproduce the colours of the hills so alien to his Bengali eyes. He was recreating a renaissance, he told the father, as he experimented with traditional art forms and formulated ponderous questions to Lalita in the Sanskritized Bengali of Calcutta intellectuals. The young neophyte painstakingly checked out each reference from her grandfather's palm leaf manuscripts, and helped him find the right herbs for his study.

His strange daughter's erudition and her great love for her surrogate painter-father awed and saddened the England-returned Brahmin. Who'd value such eccentricities here? He'd never thought a woman could see and understand so much. But then he hardly knew her—or his own father's capacity for revenge—did he? He knew he'd lost her to the old man and all the overtures he made now were going to be smashed to bits against a sullen wall of silence.

At night, when his bad heart kept him awake, Lalita's father often remembered his father's words— 'One day, when your own children cause you grief such as you've caused me, you'll remember your father.'

Ah, the curse of Brahma!

Ω   Ω   Ω

In the journey from the Vedic period to later Hinduism, Saraswati's association with her origin— the river Saraswati—gets somewhat obscured. The *Brahma Vaivarta Purana* and the *Devi Bhagvat Puranas* associate Saraswati with Krishna. She is also said to be one of the five Shaktis that emanated from the female half of Krishna. From Krishna to Vishnu is an easy passage. She's described as Vishnu's tongue, and a co-wife with Laxmi. The two are not to get on well, representing as they do *bhukta*, or sensual enjoyment, and *mukti* or liberation.

The *Vamana Purana* relinks Saraswati with the waters, but here she is described not just as a river Goddess, but the all-purifying and nourishing sap that runs through Creation.

Far more characteristic of the later Saraswati is her identification with the powers of communication. As Vac Devi (the embodiment of speech), Kavi-Jihvagravasini (she who dwells on the tip of the tongues of poets), and Mahavani (the grand speech), Saraswati is associated with the tongues of the three great Gods; and through them with the best in culture and rational communication.

♎   ♎   ♎

Lalita by now spoke many tongues.

'So what colour do you think the cows must be seen in, in the cow-dust hour?' The way Lalita answered her art teacher in fluent Bengali, and the way it all seemed to have won the father's obvious admiration, maddened her jealous cousins and siblings further. Their growls and nasty 'hunhs!', their glowering eyes and sudden silences when she entered the room, told Lalita what she already knew, that she was different and dared to be so, and for that she'd always have to pay a price.

Lalita sank more and more into silence. She took to working at night, surrounded by ancient smells and whispers. Her walks into the forest became more and more prolonged. After a while her mother took to banging pots in her kitchen and predicting aloud dire futures for over-educated daugthers whose unthinking fathers were not bothered about weeding out unfamilial ideas from their heads.

The father gazed sadly at her, but said nothing.

Lalita discovered how art, laughter and music would first alarm women like her mother and then lull them into silence. Lalita now knew exactly what she should do in case the war went on, in case the college was bombed, in case her father's anguished heart gave way. To her alone of all his children, the father had communicated that he was dying, and also that in his heart he was already a dead man.

So the college reopened and the long summer came to an end. Her father came to see her off. She said to herself, that's the way life is, Lalita, that's the way things end. She was never to see him again.

♎ ♎ ♎

Her old mentor, the bearded painter guru, consoled her with tears in his eyes when the dreaded telegram came. Silence reigned for a while. Then the guru spoke. He would be, he said, only too happy to take her on as an apprentice teacher. You must work, he said, to honour that great man. Lalita said nothing. A month later, she began to teach. Teaching served a dual purpose. She could live away and she could also send money home, and because one was linked to the other, no one could insist that she return.

Gradually, her mother, in the resigned way of simple widows with many offspring, accepted that this one had left her for good. She stopped looking for a bridegroom for her Lalita, the strange daughter born with a river-name under the sign of Capricorn. For the rest of her life Lalita was to be loved in awe and in sadness. Her mother knew there was no deliverance from the pain she carried within her, and the ascetic life she was to lead.

Never name a daughter after a river, my grand-aunt said again and again to us.

Laxmi

Deepavali, the glorious festival of lamps, and the autumnal full moon, Kojagiri Poornima, were the two days when the family worshipped Shri Laxmi specially; as Goddess of wealth and as the protector of harvests, cattle and family.

Laxmi was also worshipped in the shape of gold and silver coins and pieces of new jewellery. Platters full of fresh fruit, grains, bunches of Kadali bananas, sugarcane, lotus and *parijata* flowers were offered to her. The earth floor of the puja room was freshly cleaned and anointed, first with a coat of cow-dung, then the ochre *geru* paint, over which a series of images of tiny feet were painted like two inverted commas with a silver coin in between. These were the holy *pau*—Laxmi's auspicious footprints. They always led inside, towards the storeroom, towards the boxes, storage pots and trunks where the family wealth was stored. All night long on Deepavali day, the doors stood open and lights burnt bright, lest the short-tempered Laxmi take offence at an unwelcoming doorway and turn away.

Like most Goddesses, Laxmi was not born of a parent. She arose perfect as a pearl, out of a sea of milk, the *kshir sagara*, that the Gods and demons were churning furiously, with a mountain for a churn and a sinuous snake for the rope.

Think about it.

Laxmi reflects the system as it originally was. By piecing together the history of Laxmi and legends associated with her, we begin to see, dimly, some lost links. Much of it is history that we have been taught to overlook.

For example, when women are blessed with the words 'Be like Laxmi', it is implied that they shall be warm, generous, home-loving, but passive and obedient. But the true Laxmi is anything but meek. In her archetypal form, she is not only a creator of resources but also one who controls them with great guile and deceit whenever the need be. To be successful Laxmi needs to be clever, beguiling, bossy, and ever-mobile—not static and mute.

So Laxmi is about being ambitious and not being ashamed of it. Laxmi is about the joy of independent entrepreneurship, about risk-taking and taking the rap. The buck stops with Laxmi each time, quite literally.

We women have been told for centuries that there is something underhand, impure and even shameful about making money and working at increasing it. This mind-set crops up even among Indian feminists of both the Gandhian and Marxist variety, even while they are talking about income-generation, empowerment and economic independence of women. Yet Laxmi, the Goddess of wealth herself, is free of all that. She rises out of the sea of milk bearing riches. She is a giver from then on, never a receiver. In lore and sculpture, she negotiates, she employs tricks, she acts the coquette. If need be, she even uses her sex to advantage, and she cohabits with only those that promote and aggrandise her further. Laxmi is charismatic, beautiful and arrogant, and yes, she does not suffer fools or cowards.

Initially, no force is able to tame Laxmi's mobility as she is Chanchala, the restless one. Change occurs only when in later texts, Laxmi is married to the powerful God Vishnu, and transformed slowly into a domesticated wife. As the beloved of Vishnu, Vishnupriya, she slowly relegates all responsibility and turns placid, calm and loyal, displaying a disturbing obedience to all the social mores that had begun by then to control the lives and energies of women married to successful men. This is the Laxmi most of us were introduced to as a role model, not the original effulgent one who arose from the sea, resplendent in her self-generated resources and so totally self-sufficient and free.

In Laxmi's marriage to Vishnu and her transformation into a slavish wife massaging her sleeping husband's legs unendingly, we begin to see a story of a gradual delinking of wealth and property from women. Thereafter, Laxmi's old spirit, when it is aroused at all, reveals itself as a sharp-tongued and fractious wife, who is always quarrelling for her conjugal rights, and nagging her lord when he awakens. Or else she acts petulant and jealous of independent women, such as the celibate intellectual Saraswati. A Laxmi worrying endlessly about female competition for her ever-flirtatious lord, is a de-fanged Laxmi that men need not fear. They can lock her up and periodically permit their wives to pay obeisance to her. She is a safe role-model as a wide-hipped, bejewelled shrew. She gives and gives. And even when she takes charge, she is clever enough not to seem to be in charge.

The Story of Revati, the Prostitute

Revati lives in a Calcutta brothel. Her family lives back in her village where her mother is raising her daughter by a previous broken marriage. She regularly remits money home. For Durga and Kali Puja, during the fortnight of worship in the autumn, she sends extra money to her family to buy new clothes with. The men in her family were labourers who died young of tuberculosis. Her only brother has joined the army and never sends money home.

When men come to her and wish to chat over a beer, Revati tells them curtly that for her time is money. If they do not wish to pay extra, she'll allow them time enough to do 'it' and put their clothes on before they leave. She collects money in advance from clients and deposits it with the landlady. If she had been sold into prostitution, the landlady would have taken most of it and given her only a small pocket allowance. She was for some time an *adhiya* and shared her room rent. But now she rents her own room and a table fan, and is free to save what she can.

Revati's mother has told the villagers that her daughter works in Calcutta as a maidservant. The villagers nod knowingly. Most young girls in the village have been 'sent' to Calcutta as maids. They all remit money home regularly. The boys, however, once they've left for the city, are seldom seen again.

Ω   Ω   Ω

The real Laxmi is a Goddess we have largely been taught to forget. She is not a conduit for passing power on to children (read sons and sons-in-law). Laxmi herself has no children. Strange, when you come to think of it, that the Goddess of riches and fertility should be so noticeably childless. But as I said earlier, most of us were taught not to notice many aspects of the Laxmi myths. Laxmi denies inheritance and continuity of wealth consciously, and

always. She is Chanchala—the ever-mobile one—
who stays with only those who can retain her.

Ω   Ω   Ω

In the earliest Vedic texts the Goddess appears as
Sri, meaning glory. Sri also stands for beauty, ruling
power and majesty such as kings have.

The Tale of the Moneylender, Savitriakka

Fifty-year-old Savitriakka is the childless widow of
the village headman who died ten years ago. At the
time of her marriage, her husband owned more than
twenty-four acres of land in Konur. After his death
she sold the land through her nephews who, she
claims, defrauded her. She now mistrusts men, male
relatives in particular. She thinks they are eyeing
her money, and she's mostly right. They are a good-
for-nothing lot, she says, who chew betelnut and get
drunk in the evenings and refuse to work. She
prefers her nieces whom she brought up and married
off with gold jewellery worth fifteen *pawans*.

Savitriakka's income is now through interest
receipts from money lent out. She has a bank account
in a Dindigul bank where she has also rented a vault
for her gold jewellery. Her house is another source
of pride to her. Built by her late husband, it is
strong, well-made and has a tiled roof. She was, till
her husband's death, actively involved in community
development projects in her village. As a widow, she
can no longer be. She is still an articulate woman
with strong opinions, though, and commands a lot of

respect in her village, even though she has no husband or son.

♎   ♎   ♎

Vishnu had bagged Laxmi early. Lore has it that as Laxmi arose out of the sea of milk, bearing a red lotus in her hand, each member of the divine triad— Brahma, Vishnu and Shiva—wanted to have her for himself. Shiva's claim was refused for he had already claimed the Moon. So Vishnu claimed her and she was born and reborn as his consort during all of his ten incarnations.

In my grandmother's puja room, there was a silver idol of Vishnu, inset with a small piece of gold.

'Why is that?'

'It is Laxmi, she is gold.'

Mother said that Laxmi, together with Vishnu, were Gods of all the good things of life.

Among the many pictures that lined the walls of Grandmother's puja room, one of the largest depicted Gaja-Laxmi in regal splendour, flanked by two elephants anointing her with holy water that gushed out of their raised trunks. Her hair was long and lustrous and from her palms, a stream of gold coins fell into the waters at her feet. The picture had a lot of gold in it. The crown on Laxmi's head was gold, also her jewellery and the flecks upon her bright red sari. There was no idol of hers, but on each Deepavali day, a new silver coin and a piece of gold jewellery were worshipped as Laxmi. Before this ritual the entire puja platform was cleaned and plastered over with fresh cow-dung. Cleanliness, we were told, was a fetish with Laxmi. If she visited a house that had not been cleaned and painted properly, she'd return and send her mean sister A-Laxmi, who'd bring penury, illness and quarrels to the house.

As children from a ritualistic Brahmin household, we were taught early that earth and cow-dung were dear to Laxmi. They were not to be regarded as dirty or smelly, but holy and purifying. Mud may look dirty, but it was only there that the lotus bloomed and the *navadhanya*, the new grain, sprouted its dainty shoots in the ritual pots. Come each nine-day festival of Navratri, Laxmi was thus to us, both mud and lotus, cow-dung and frothy nourishing milk.

☋   ☋   ☋

The *Shri-Sukta* in Vedic literature, which appears as part of an appendix to the *Rig Veda*, depicts Laxmi as moist and fertile, perceptible through odour. She has the mysterious potency of freshly turned and irrigated earth.

The fifteen verses of the *Shri-Sukta*, appended to the fifth book of the *Rig Veda*, describe Laxmi's beauty and bounty, which are referred to in other old texts as well. She is described as Kamala and Kamalanana, of the colour of a pink lotus, surrounded by red lotuses, a bestower of gold and cattle and a guardian of health, harvest, beauty and fame. The *Shukla Yajur Veda* depicts Laxmi and Shri as two wives of the sun God Aditya, while the *Shatpath Brahmana* tells us that she is a creation of Brahma or Prajapati. The *Aitareya Brahmin* describes her as earth, rich, fertile and steady.

Laxmi is also sex, independent of maternity. She is not your average rustic belle singing lustily in the fields, though. As Shri, she has the tremendous arrogance of nobility. It is said she enjoys the company of men who are noble, regal and aggressive. But she cannot abide those that do not exude breeding, do not wear good, clean clothes, comb their hair properly or eat gracefully. She hates uncouth behaviour of all kinds and would rather reside with demons like Bali who have the sophistication and the regal bearing of a leader. She may let vulgar idiots pirouette giddily in front of her, but she withdraws neatly at the first opportunity. In her frosty disdain for commoners, she is as exact as a gold sovereign.

My Friend X

X was by no means a young girl when I met her. She was a small, slender, lustrous-haired millionairess in her thirties and an unusual beauty, with a wide forehead, a mouth with thin mistrusting lips and a soft receding chin. She sat surrounded by an aura of expensive perfume in a decaying mansion, fussed over constantly by old family retainers and greying managers. They were helping her settle in her family business of publishing. The old building was littered with discarded machinery, enormous rolls of imported newsprint and the smell of cat and human urine mixed with petrol fumes. Depressed after her parents' death, X apparently had to be coaxed and cajoled to come and sit in the offices she had inherited from her grandfather. She was fussy about cleanliness and discipline and the building notably lacked both. It was out of this malodorous and rich chaos, she should know, that the family millions had blossomed in the last half-century, her aunt, the matriarch of the family, had told her. She was the one who managed to bring her here after everyone else had failed.

X both loved and loathed her aunt. But her aunt was right.

Money is power. Writers, editors, crooks, all entered X's room on tiptoe, trying to put a jaunty face on their masculine embarrassment at having to fetch and carry for a chit of a girl. X, the aunt had decreed, must meet them all with an impressive face. Occasionally running her beautiful hands over her auburn tresses, X drove the men wild with desire and sorrow. Once outside her room, most of them would let on that they were doing something they really despised, and that she was just a rich bitch, a spoilt brat. But their flat and angry tones belied their real feelings.

How's your magazine, X asked me once when she saw me looking thoughtful. I said work was fine but I would have liked a little more of everything, work, money, elbow space, privacy of thought. But somehow I seemed to rub everyone the wrong way. Frequently, I didn't know what I was doing there at those interminable meetings to decide the literary prize of the year.

X smiled and let it go at that. 'Why don't you come for the formal dinner tomorrow? My aunt is having a party. Join us?' she asked casually as I got up to leave. 'Frankly, I'm sick of her awards and her literary lions. I'd like to see writers like you more often,' she added.

I was foolish and vain and young and of course, deeply flattered. I went. No sooner had I stepped into the house I knew I had been stupid to have come. This was a house where all that entered had to surrender their power and their will at the massive wrought-iron gates. And once in, you hung around waiting to catch the hostess' eye. You bloomed like a lotus when she shone her light upon you, you wilted when she passed you by. In the meanwhile, you sipped tepid fruit juice, looked at possible rivals through the corner of your eyes, and you waited.

It was a beautiful living room panelled in raw silk, inset with leaves from rare manuscripts and illustrations. All the writers and artists the aunt had got to crowd in seemed somewhat out of place in these opulent surroundings. Writers, editors, art critics, dancers, musicians, painters, all stood around drinking fruit juice and eating out of trays of food circulated by cat-footed bearers. We avoided eye-contact with each other as we simpered and fawned.

Once outside we bitched about the award and the awardees.

♎   ♎   ♎

The aunt rose from the stark white raw silk sofa like a lotus. She was wrapped in an earth-coloured silk sari, resplendent with family jewels. She was fair, Junoesque and a little too erect in the way of those who spend a good part of their mornings standing on their head or palms or whatever, in intricate yogic postures.

'I know who you are,' she said patting me on my back with her bejewelled fingers, 'but I thought you looked older on TV.' People said this to me occasionally, perhaps because of the terrible make-up they made you wear in Doordarshan studios and the uncomfortable chairs they sat you in, after which you had no choice but to slouch, scowl and look serious. I wanted to be a witty genius whose stern exterior belied her innate good humour and love of fun. I was somewhat hurt when people refused to go beyond the screen persona and took me for what I thought I was not.

The aunt peered closely at me as though I were an exotic pebble, as only the very rich and the very eccentric can. 'You are very busy, aren't you? I see you so often on TV talk shows and I notice you do columns as well. How do you find the time?' The sensuous mouth on her austere nun-like face pouted with feigned wonder. While I was fishing for a profound and amusing reply, she suddenly waved to someone across the room and moved on.

Just moved on.

My disappointment, my rage and, above all, my envy, were indescribable. I must not be reckless, I reminded myself, I was in the home of my employer. I must get through the evening without betraying my feelings. As I grappled with desperate alternatives, the aunt suddenly turned and directed a smile of such fulness and pleasure at me that I was transported. All was forgiven. Well, almost.

Then suddenly her niece, my friend X, was at my elbow in a crumpled home-laundered T-shirt and trousers that had seen better days. The aunt whizzed by, 'Darling, is that all you could find to wear?' She chucked X under the chin and flashed another smile, aiming it conspiratorially at me.

X scowled at her and bit her nails.

The frustrations of the day, the grand snub delivered by the aunt, the background chatter, the smell of spicy snacks and now this encounter between the two women, left me feeling somewhat disoriented.

'I see that you've already been cut dead and resurrected by the Laxmi of the house?' X said when the aunt was out of sight. Her brown eyes were now sparkling with laughter.

'Yes. She is nice.'

I was still thinking of the big smile.

'That's something she is definitely not.'

'She's very beautiful,' I persisted.

'Yes. I can see that she's flashed her forget-me-not smile at you.'

'But she has a beautiful smile.'

'I don't wish to hear more about her.'

X stalked off suddenly to speak to an artist who nearly fell over in ecstasy at the honour. Rudeness had to be their family trait.

I felt odd and useless hanging around. I could see the aunt weave in and out of the crowd like a diamond needle. Then I lost her.

'So you don't like your aunt,' I said to X. We sat outside in the garden surrounded by priceless antique statues. There was a cool breeze and she looked thin and miserable and lost in the vast gardens.

'I don't care one way or the other,' she said, 'she wants to possess everything and everyone. Even enter their dreams if she can. Do you know she asked me to write down what qualities I wanted in my husband-to-be, and each time I rejected a suitor, I was to send her a note giving at least four good reasons why I did that.'

'What's wrong with that? It shows she cares for you, doesn't it?'

'She just wants everything,' X got up and fetched herself a glass of some fruity drink. 'You look miserable. How would you like me to have your office shifted to the other building?'

I hesitated.

I didn't know how to refuse this sudden generosity without offending her. It was clear she was extending a hand in friendship, but I was hesitant all the same. Like her, I too did not want to be possessed. Also she would never know how really unhappy I was working at the outfit. It was worse than she'd ever know. Locked up in her wood-panelled, perfumed and air-conditioned office, she'd never know the cruel sea of depravity and greed that pushed us out towards the dry beach, all the time, like gritty and broken sea-shells. You had to be a Laxmi to survive the sea. I was a writer and an uncouth hill-woman, a foreigner upon her shores.

'I'll think about it,' I mumbled.

At the workplace, X's growing warmth towards me depressed me more than the hostility it aroused in my colleagues and superiors. She was my only

friend in the grim building with peeling walls, and
frankly I had nowhere else to go. But I was loath to
accept this. My husband was between two uncertain
jobs, my children were in a school that guzzled most
of our meagre savings. The only certain and constant
factor in my life at that point was my writing and I
was sure that neither the aunt nor X herself had
ever read a word of it.

A vast alien sea and a vernacular language
separated us. The sea was their natural element but
I had to kick all the time, even to stay afloat. And
I was tired of doing that after four years.

℥   ℥   ℥

It was a long drive home from X's home to mine.
The drive through the empty roads lined with trees
that hid the houses of the wealthy, helped calm me
down. Certainly their interests and praise never
ceased to flatter me, but it also filled me with a
certain guilt. 'Sorry,' I often said aloud to no one in
particular.

℥   ℥   ℥

X was out when I sent in my resignation. I broke the
news to her on the phone. 'You are right, it's no
place for you. I wouldn't want to come back either,
if I didn't have to.'

Two years later X was dead.

She escaped quietly, with no farewell. To me she
sent a bundle of her favourite books, wrapped in
coarse paper and tied with an old shoelace.

Some sense of humour that.
Some farewell.

℥   ℥   ℥

Tradition also associates Laxmi with Kubera, the ugly lord of the Yakshas. The Yakshas were a race of supernatural creatures, who lived outside the pale of civilization. Their connection with Laxmi perhaps springs from the fact that they were notable for a propensity for collecting, guarding and distributing wealth. Association with Kubera deepens the aura of mystery and underworld connections that attaches itself to Laxmi. Yakshas are also symbolic of fertility. The Yakshinis depicted often in temple sculpture are full-breasted and big-hipped women with wide generous mouths, leaning seductively against trees.

In Almora there is a temple to Jakhani Debi (Yakshini Devi). Women pray to her for a child. 'A boy or a girl?' I once asked Khyali, our old family retainer. 'Boy of course,' he bellowed in his gritty phlegmatic voice. 'Are they mad to pray for a daughter? It is only when you produce a son that the *pitaras*—the divine ancestors—accept you and give you power.'

℥   ℥   ℥

Laxmi enters the Vaishnava school of devotion as Lord Vishnu's demure consort, but she soon takes it over. In the *Panchratra* school of thought, Laxmi becomes the true power—Shakti—of Vishnu. Having married her, Vishnu delegates the supervision of creation to his powerful consort Laxmi, and himself

goes to sleep on his *sheshshaiyaa*—the snake bed—
in the sea of milk. Laxmi acts by herself, as she
deems fit. It is she who thus becomes the true
granter of desires and saviour of souls.

*Like the fat that helps the lamp burn, I keep awake
the senses of living beings with my own sap.*

(Laxmi Tantra 50:110
—a popular Panchratra text)

Vishnu, to Vaishnavites is an awesome God;
transcendent and somewhat unapproachable. As his
wife, Shri Laxmi also becomes the divine mediator
who intercedes with the Lord on behalf of the lowly
devotees. She thus brings to Vishnu's court an
intimacy and warmth that considerably softens our
awed vision of the divine.

☊   ☊   ☊

Dear Mother, some day when the time is right.
   *Please remind the Lord of me, after broaching the
subject of human misery . . .*
   Thus petitions the saint—the poet Tulsidas.

☊   ☊   ☊

Laxmi is the protector of crops and food. A full
granary, abundant harvest, an aromatic kitchen
overflowing with milk, butter and yoghurt, are all
considered her boon. And this means that profligate
spending, orgies, gluttony and boisterous gambling
would also be associated with her as a matter of
course. Deepavali, the festival of lamps, is the time

when Laxmi's worshippers give in to excesses of every kind. Interestingly, during this festival Laxmi is worshipped together with, not her usual consort Vishnu, but Ganesha. All over the north, clay idols of Laxmi and Ganesha are sold before Deepavali, to be worshipped on the auspicious day. Ganesha again is a Yaksha-like figure, fat, smart and associated with wealth and good luck.

Laxmi as Chanchala, or the mobile one, associates only with the rich and the dynamic, no matter what their caste, creed or colour. As such, even the demons Bali and Prahlada, who fulfil the above qualifications, are graced with her company. While she resides with them, their kingdom prospers, crops bloom, the royal coffers overflow with money, the monsoons bring thick clouds and plentiful rain. When she moves out of their palaces (at the request of the fair Aryan god Indra or Vishnu), they lose their lustre and good fortune and go into decline. Vishnu tricks Bali into surrendering the three worlds to him, with active collaboration from Laxmi. Once Bali loses his riches, Laxmi moves out on him.

Her fickleness and adventurous nature slowly begin to change, once she is identified totally with Vishnu, and finally becomes still. She then becomes the steadfast, obedient and loyal wife who vows to reunite with her husband in all his next lives. As the cook at the Jagannatha temple in Puri, she prepares food for her lord and his devotees. She is now mostly depicted with two arms instead of the usual four. In the famous paintings on the walls of the Badami caves in central India, she sits on the ground near where her lord reclines upon a throne, leaning on him; a model of social decorum and correctitude.

The Mother-in-law

Up there is the loft in the old house, there is a box of old photographs. In them Mother-in-law sits on a chair, flanked by her sons. Father-in-law stands beside her in his three-piece suit and gleaming shoes. Mother-in-law's face is round and wide, her mouth, coloured bright by the photographer, is in a correct line. She wears much gold, many pearls and carries a Japanese fan.

The husband's career ended too soon. But not before she could build a new house. They sold off the family car and retired to the house. It is a huge house and requires constant supervision. The servants cheat and lie and need to be shouted at all the time.

She often tells her daughters-in-law, they'll realize the worth of property only when she is gone. They serve her with the sorrowful patience of mothers with sons of their own, their eyes gleam with hopes of division and rebuilding.

'Come quick,' says Mother-in-law to the family at night. She points at the Very Important Persons on the television screen. Sometimes they turn down the volume so as not to wake up the grandsons and watch the parade of VIPs go by. The mother-in-law's voice quavers when she describes to the family days of her glory when her husband too was a VIP. Often, she cries as she remembers. No one is quite sure what exactly she is sorry about. Her husband has been faithful and a good provider. Now he usually dozes after a meal, full of shadowy memories of a certain steel frame, long since gone. They created the nation with Nehru, he tells the sons often. They pretend to listen deferentially.

Mother-in-law roams the house, constantly casting furtive glances at her married sons' rooms and their wives, assessing the weight of gold on their torsoes and wondering if they are pregnant.

'You look pale and tired,' she tells the sons frequently.

'They look better than ever,' retort the wives.

'You are not being fed well,' says Mother-in-law. She sighs meaningfully. The house is full of her aromatic cooking. 'Mother, we have to go,' say the sons. They pat their mother's shoulders with lovers' hands. Even now her hair is dark, fragrant and hangs to her waist when she washes it.

In the afternoon, other mothers-in-law drop by. Then they all go to the temple of the Goddess, to sing hymns.

'Where are the old men?' the grandson asks the grandfather.

'I think they've died. We men go off quicker,' the grandfather laughs.

'Or maybe they only sleep, like you?'

'Yes, maybe they do too.'

Then the grandfather lies down and dozes and the grandson goes out to play.

Ω　　Ω　　Ω

It was a Deepavali day. The older son had just been married. Mother-in-law made the bride wear all her ancestral jewellery. She herself was resplendent with her face half covered with the ancestral nose-ring threaded with pearls and emeralds. Together they invoked Laxmi, with lamps, fruits, sweets, incense and flowers. They were all dressed in new clothes that rustled as only thick new silk can. As the father and sons waved the prayer lamps around, the mother-in-law and the daughter-in-law rang the bell and blew the conchshell.

The room was full of light, of rustling silk, of gold and silver and incense fumes.

Ω Ω Ω

Mother-in-law's face is hard, sensual hard, as she distributes the holy offerings mixed with *jai* flowers. 'Take it into your right palm, not the left,' she says curtly to the giggly daughter-in-law whose husband is looking at her as men look at women.

Later she is to tell the daughter-in-law about the trust her father-in-law had offered to set up for her first-born, of which she is to be the executor provided that it is a male child. Her large eyes dilate as she describes the sum of money, multiplying over the years. It's best for a woman to marry money and produce sons, she tells the daughter-in-law. 'Men may not have our stamina, but they have the money,' she sniffs and lifts her chin, 'never forget that'.

Inside, Father-in-law sleeps on the huge four-poster with frilly pillows. His fingers move as though he wants to clutch at the air. The keys to the store and the family safe hang in a bunch on Mother-in-law's ample waist with a silver hook.

Money multiplies in the name of the grandson.

The daughter-in-law smiles. She is the executor.

It has been a perfect passing down of powers from the old Laxmi to the new.

The men sleep. The grandson plays.

The women guard them like gold.

The Earth Mother

In the Earth Mother, qualities of Saraswati and Laxmi mix and mutate.

According to the sacred *Brahmana* texts, in the beginning there was only a grey, windless cloud. Then Prajapati, the Creator, undertook great austerities and released an immense store of energy. This ball of energy went on to form the cosmos. As Dyava Prithivir, they were an inseparable whole: earth mother and father sky. Together they went on to sire powerful progeny: Indra and Agni, wind and fire. Then Varuna came and parted them and they thus became two separate entities, one female, the other male: Prithvi and Dyavs. As a mother, earth began to acquire a persona of her own: stable, fecund and moist, inexhaustibly feeding the millions that lived off her.

May earth, always protected by the
Ceaseless care of Gods that never sleep,
Pour out for us delicious
Nectar, may she bedew
Us with a flood of splendour.

(Atharva Veda)

Prithvi, as the divine feminine, represented all that was both sacred and also profane; temporal as well as immortal—like life itself. The word *mitti*, or earth, has since been synonymous with flesh in most Indian languages; and the potter that shaped it was Prajapati or Vishwakarma, creator of the world. In Hindi, earth as *mitti* or *mati* is said to outlive the Creator. Thus said the weaver poet Kabir:

Mati kahe kumhar se, tu kya roonde moye
Ek din aisa ayega, main roondoongi toye

'Says earth to the Potter, you can't crush and knead me for ever. A day shall come when I shall be kneading you.'

Identification of the cerebral Goddess with the immortal and all-sustaining earth, is followed naturally by identifying various objects on this earth with parts of her body. The *Devi Bhagavatpurana* calls the earth the Goddess' loins, the mountains her breasts, the oceans her bowels and the trees, her tresses. In Manipur, the Mother Goddess, Panthoibi, is still the patron-Goddess of all potters. She is said to have handed the gift of pot-making to the women of Manipur.

The flesh-mind duality is underscored further by one of the names given to mother earth: Medini, she that is composed of fat. Legend has it that when Vishnu, as Narayana, killed the twin monsters Madhu and Kaitabh, their cumulative fat, *meda*, formed an enormous mound out of which the earth was created. The *Atharva Veda* immortalised this image in hymns that sang of Prithvi as *bhumi* or land that yielded a steady supply of nourishing and rejuventating food, and also provided a steady warmth to millions of its children.

Like most generous and passive givers, Medini was soon to learn about greed and exploitation. According to legend, all her children, both the nomads and the settlers, chose to exploit her. First it was the sage Kashyapa's son Hiranyaksh, the golden-eyed bully. King Bhuvana's son, Vishwakarma, foolishly also took Medini's generous passivity as proof of her subjugation by man, so he promised to give her away to Kashyapa, and after him to his son, Hiranyaksh. 'No mortal can ever give me away,' cried the gentle Medini. She appealed to the Gods that they stop the obnoxious practice of buying and selling her, saying that she felt deeply humiliated by such greed. But the fierce Kashyapa family had terrorised everyone, including the Gods. All Medini received from the divine pantheon, was a deafening silence.

To escape the nomadic marauders, Medini is said ultimately to have dived into the oceans and stayed there till Vishnu as the boar Varaha rescued her. Then Vena, the wayward son of one of the forefathers of the human race, Anga Prajapati, arrived on the scene. He forbade worship and sacrifice and began harassing the gentle, bountiful Medini once again, urging her to give more and more. At this Medini was filled with rage. She retaliated by suddenly becoming infertile. The rains stopped, crops withered, rivers dried up. Enraged by hunger and deprivations, the sages eventually killed Vena and replaced him with Prithu.

Prithu put a stop to the suicidal march of the nomads and levelled the ground with his bow, making the land fit for cultivation. Having tamed his savage subjects and settled them into an agricultural cycle, as farmers and cattle-breeders, King Prithu asked Medini to relent and become a provider again. But he had over-estimated his powers and underestimated Medini's wrath. He was aggressive and rude and that angered Medini further. But she knew the power of Prithu's bow. To escape his arrows, Medini cunningly turned herself into a holy cow, and chided Prithu petulantly for harassing a sacred milch animal. She'd give, she said, but first Prithu must ask Manu, the prevailing leader of mankind, to turn into a calf and milk her udders naturally, painlessly. Only then would her nourishing generosity be available to the sinful mortals, and the long drought be over.

Kindness and gentle handling were needed here, and Prithu turned out to be an intelligent learner. What Medini wished was done and Prithu went on to adopt her as his daughter. Hence her name, Prithvi.

A variant of this legend however, relates that Prithu, the son of Vishnu, married the earth, Prithvi. But she, finding him wanting in grace, refused to yield all her treasures to him. As she withheld her bounty, a terrible famine ensued. In his anger Prithu wanted to kill Prithvi, who changed herself into a sacred cow to evade being killed, and ran for protection to Brahma. Brahma, in the manner of many Indian fathers, refused to shelter her against her husband's wrath and ordered her to return to Prithu. Upon her return, Prithvi was severely beaten and made to yield her treasures under duress.

Prithvi's exploitation and her scheming revenge, her ambivalence towards her husband and children, her rage at being sold piecemeal and her need for kindness are the basic features of all earthly love. Mothers must love their children and wives their husbands. This is one of the most commonly held beliefs in all civilizations that have been created and run by men. Earth's story, as she changed from passive Medini to a scheming cow and then to gentle Prithvi, counters this belief. It reveals how good mothers may generally be treated in male-centric civilizations as weak, dependent and somewhat bovine, and how they may then use feminine guile to withold nourishing love. As Medini struggles with the ambivalence of the withholding of her fertility, while simultaneously being kind and gentle and generous, she discovers that the greedy among her children are beginning to exploit her. She then allows herself to hate as well as to love. Over and above everything else, Medini realizes that mankind is a survivor. It shall survive both her love and hate. What it cannot survive however, is the opposite of a mother's love, which is not hate, but a cessation of feeling.

As she decides not to disenchant her exploiters, or defy the royal bow of Prithu, Prithvi discovers how the panther-prowl of all-devouring greed may be stalled by just freezing over and hiding her treasures.

And thus passive resistance was born.

Ω   Ω   Ω

Medha Patkar is a small woman, with prematurely greyed hair, yet her name strikes terror in the heart of the lobbyists for big dams in modern India. For the last decade this frail woman has squatted patiently by the side of the river Narmada to uphold the cause of hundreds of tribals who, she claims, will be ousted from their homes if the proposed big dam over the river is built. She is hated by politicians in the three mighty states of Gujarat, Maharashtra and Madhya Pradesh. 'That cow!' says the cross-eyed minister to us, as we plead with him to save the fasting Medha's life and order a halt to the work on the dam. 'She is nothing but trouble. I should have thought you journalists would be better-employed looking for a believable story elsewhere; from among our irrigation department engineers, for example. Do you know that vast stretches of the canal are ready, but this woman will not permit water to run into it? It is because of her that the

World Bank has withdrawn its funding for our project.'

At night Medha and her supporters from all over the country sleep curled up in the chill. Crops are withering in Gujarat, cash crops, she is told!

She smiles a small cold smile, perfect as a sickle.

How Aunt Lalita Became a Mother

Aunt Lalita, as a celibate teacher, aged thirty-two, was remitting money home regularly. The women had begun re-embellishing the strange and generous daughter's virtues to the neighbours. But just as they began describing her as a nun married to her Art and Learning, Aunt Lalita announced her plans to get married. Her sisters felt she did this so she could outrage them all over again. In a way they were not wholly wrong. Lalita knew how a sudden reversal of plans would bother the family, by now dependent on her money orders immeasurably and constantly. She also knew how outraged they would be if she gave up her job, stopped the regular contributions, selected a strange outsider with one lung for a fiance, flirted with him publically and then married him in a civil ceremony in a court.

She was right on all counts.

It was a late marriage by all standards. After the marriage, the couple moved to Vishnupur, a sleepy little hill-town shaped like a horse saddle, where a motor road rose and ran over and around the hills like a sacred thread.

For nearly half-a-century, Aunt Lalita was to live in this picturesque small town, named after the God who loved cows, who was the protector of Laxmi and who also slept most of the time. He was said to have been kicked in the chest by the sage Bhrigu, and carried the footprint of death on his chest.

Vishnupur's only claim to fame was a veterinary research institute, founded sometime in the nineteenth century by the British. It produced internationally famed vaccines for poultry against a dreaded epidemic disease called *ranikhet*, and for milch cattle against an equality horrible malady, foot-and-mouth disease. The serums for the vaccines were prepared in a culture of equine blood, for which the institute maintained a surprisingly fine stable of well-bred horses. Vishnupur's mixture of high science and low comedy, sickness and health, learning and lethargy, suited my aunt's new plans for motherhood perfectly.

A change of image was called for now. Aunt Lalita attired herself to fit the image of an all-bountiful mother. To this end she gave up those coarse white khadi saris and demure long-sleeved cholis, and began to overdress with a vengeance. Even those who knew nothing of the feminine art of make-up could discern something totally unorthodox and larger-than-life in her exaggerated application of the traditional items of feminine cosmetics. The kohl lines framed her eyes like goggles, her *bindi* was a big dot the size of a rupee coin, and her feet, which were outlined with magenta *alta* dye, that left all the bedsheets in the house tinged with a faint pink, always tinkled with elaborate silver anklets. She also recklessly wore a great assortment of traditional jewellery from all over India. Necklaces made from Nepali corals, strings of jade from Tibet, *mangalsutras* from Maharashtra, gold chains from Kerala and gold *kanpasha* earrings from Bengal.

The creamy layer of Vishnupur society, which Lalita had to tackle first, consisted of a pantheon of British officials and scientists that ran the institute, a few Indian officials of the forest department who were mostly away touring and, of course, the good doctor, Lalita's noble husband, who served as a bridge between the whites and the non-whites. They even had a club that was a pucca *adda* for the *sahibs* to which entry was forbidden to all non-whites save the doctor. It had a full-fledged bar lined with framed cartoons from *Punch*, excellent tennis courts, and last but not the least, an enormous ball room with the finest wooden parquet flooring.

The doctor was a handsome man with sharp acquiline features, a most beautiful smile and the dainty hands and feet of an angel. He dressed well, in Western clothes, and like the *sahibs*, maintained a cook and bearer who alternately cooked him Indian and Western-style food. He'd refused to return earlier to his native town, he said, for fear of being polluted by those uncivilized and uncouth boors of the hills, who wiped their snot on their fingers and washed their arses after defaecating.

The doctor was a local boy orphaned early in life who had dazzled the town in his early days with his remarkable power of mind and body but had disappeared beyond its horizons having gone on to graduate in medicine from England. The people of the town heard with a sort of vague interest about the many gold medals and certificates that he had won and how he had gone on to become something of a celebrated dandy, first in the *nawabi* and thereafter in the Edwardian tradition.

All of a sudden one winter, the doctor, while still in England, was struck with the dreaded TB in his lungs. He had to have an operation and one of his lungs was sealed off completely. His fellow-surgeons, who operated on him, advised him to go back to the pine-scented hills in India if he wished to survive with one lung in the tropics, and avoid the Second World War. So the doctor, with a freshly-healed scar on his chest, applied to the Government Hospital in Vishnupur for the post of a medical superintendent and was promptly accepted. Having taken charge of the hospital, he decided to pay his hometown a visit, he never could explain why. It was the Venus

Mahadasha in his horoscope, said his mother-in-law later, that had nudged him thither, for it was the same town where Aunt Lalita grew up, and was then visiting. Anyway, one day, while Lalita was walking down the road to the pine forests of Shitoli with her bag of hand-made Nepali paper and bottles of rare herbal colours and brushes, she was said to have chanced upon this exotic young fop being carried in a palanquin with the equanimity of a young nawab. He was twirling an ivory-tipped cane, and was dressed in a three-piece suit. He tipped his felt hat to her, as she passed by, and though she scowled at him haughtily, when she sat down to paint in the forest that day, instead of drawing the trees and the creepers, she drew scenes from Kalidas' *Kumarsambhavan*, of Aparna Parvati doing a special *tapas* to get her Shiva as a husband, of Laxmi and Vishnu courting and dancing, of two doves locked in a kiss upon a rhododendron tree.

The doctor had apparently found her equally unforgettable, what with her weird clothes, her open and friendly eyes and that tall and well-built frame. In an area where both women and cows were unusually small, pale and passive, she of the tall and lissom frame, with her ample breasts and childbearing hips, drew him to her effortlessly. He had found what he had been looking for all these years, and although she had no intentions of giving anyone her consent, Lalita gave him hers.

They had a brief courtship and then married.

Because she was a woman learned in the scriptures, and a good astrologer, Aunt Lalita had naturally to begin her married life by acting devout. But her brand of devotion was, like everything about her, unique and self-created. Her reverence found shape in poems and the serving of holy food. Twice a year she fasted for nine days when the two nine-day Navratri cycles began. During those nine days she cooked non-stop, inventing ingenious substitutes for grain, which was forbidden, from the kingdom of tubers. From the dry potato-farming soil of the terraced fields next to their house, Lalita produced sacks full of starchy roots, plump as the moon. She herself began to grow round and full. Each season saw a fresh layer of fat cover an already well-covered body. Her ample breasts grew into veritable mounds, her hips spread out and then jutted out like the chassis of a truck.

'Red is the colour of married bliss, of *suhag!*' Lalita explained with a laugh to somewhat puzzled first-time visitors to the red interiors of her nest. To surround herself and her house with accepted icons and symbols of marital love, of *suhag*, wasn't that what a Hindu woman was supposed to do? No one could find fault with that.

Then Lalita gradually began altering known rituals that had made her dependent on male priests. She banished the family Gods to a small room next to the kitchen, where a succession of old Brahmin cooks bathed them ritualistically each day. She explained how her long, unclean periods of unpredictable menstruation made it imperative that the holy idols be handled by the Brahmin cook. Her visits to their room grew perfunctory and absent-minded. Having made sure that the Gods had been relegated to the limitless beyond, Lalita turned aside to discuss with the cook the meals they were to serve in the house for the next half-a-century.

Thus grew a world Lalita had assembled in her own fashion, piece by piece, curtain by curtain, cushion by cushion, pouffe by pouffe, love-seat by love-seat. Here she would rule with an iron hand, permitting no substitute for the reverence that was her due. Even time would move her only when she wished it to. History would be catalogued and frozen, till she wished to thaw it out. And so, nothing that came out of the inside of this house would ever be thrown away. All records were to be stored in a series of small tar-coated tin sheds, that surrounded her large garden like a miniature shanty-town. In one of these tin-made rooms, boxes of photographs would be kept in neat piles. All tin trunks, filing cabinets, and book racks would be painted a bright green. The stored goods within these ramshackle, but always tightly sealed, rooms were to be the only evidence of passing time and the family was to return again and again to consult the photographs, periodicals and letters filed neatly therein. These, however, were never to be permitted back inside the house. Each packet was to bear, in parrot-green ink in Aunt Lalita's beautiful calligraphic script, a neat account of what it held within.

Nothing, but nothing, was able hereafter to pry loose the grip of those plump fingers with their upturned tips upon the house where she was to spawn and share and shape many, many lives.

The first child arrived within ten months and was a girl. Punya—good deeds—they called her. Later, Lalita was to tell her children again and again how beautiful and well-formed and perfect she was, till the widowed aunt that lived down the hill came visiting and surreptitiously left a lemon with vermilion markings tucked under the baby's mustard-seed pillow. From that day Punya had stopped drinking her milk and began vomiting out whatever was fed her. She began to lose weight moreover, by the hour. Her loud wails slowly became soft mewlings and then quieted further into soundless twitches. With one such last twitch, the baby died.

It is not true, as some in the family may tell you, that after the baby's demise Lalita lost heart and became something of a religiously-inclined loner.

Once she had cleared her mind of sorrow and put her thoughts in order, Aunt Lalita began a long wait for the conception of a male child. She insisted on a male because Punya, her female child, had let her down by dying. For a start, she took to sitting in her fertile gardens where a myriad plants were always blooming, withering and dropping seed; where cats of all colours growled in the heat, mated, reproduced, shed or grew a thick new coat. She felt, she said, strong currents of maternal sap run up her legs as she stood surveying so much fertility. She was young, well rounded, had menstruated copiously and had a young and lusty husband. Why then, each month, did her menstrual blood flow out and stretch the wait longer?

Shouldn't she now ask the Gods personally for help, she thought. Not to wage a war against the elements, but just to settle a few disagreeable details?

So Aunt Lalita began to make exotic offerings to the Gods. She produced at great cost from far-away plains, coconuts with smooth wet insides like a young woman's uterus. She offered another rarity in the hills: bunches of Kadali bananas. She offered whole bunches to the Gods of this succulent, mouth-filling and firm fruit, intriguingly threaded with silky veins that tickled the insides of the mouth. She also took to fasting each Monday in the month of Shravana, the monsoon month so dear to the Gods.

The year was 1944.

One particularly auspicious Monday in Shravana was set aside to make one thousand and one *Shivalingams* out of cow-dung. This was for a special puja that was as abstract as the logic behind a woman's desires. Lalita read out to the old priest a *shloka* from some old palm-leaf manuscript, which said if you wanted prosperity you should make the *lingams* out of clay, if you wanted a husband for your daughter, you should make them with thickened milk. But if you wanted a son and heir, then you must make one thousand and one *lingams* with cow-dung and bathe them with the holy water from the river Ganges on the auspicious day in the month of Shravana. Preparations for the puja began in earnest.

The doctor never visited the puja room, but on the day of this puja he had agreed to sit at the dining table in the room next door. He would, he said, go in only at the end when the final offerings were to be made. He sat quietly and drank chilled beer out of a silver tankard as he listened abstractedly to the holy chants from within. Kheemoo, his old retainer, massaged his dainty ankles and cracked his knuckles in the meanwhile.

♎   ♎   ♎

The puja gathers momentum.

The chants begin to rise. Fumes of *aguru* incense float in. As he drinks, the salty froth lingers on the doctor's moustache. He sips softly, listening to his wife and the priest coax his seed into her barren womb with strange *mantras*, invoked with the sweet ringing of silver bells. *Bilva* leaves and cow-dung *lingams*, jauntily capped with wholegrain rice, are being bathed with holy water mixed with milk, honey and yoghurt. His tongue darts out wetly, and the doctor licks the saline froth upon his moustache again and again.

Lalita is glimpsed briefly, her face glistening with warm sweat and hunger. 'Come,' she says simply, 'come,' to her husband when the time for the final offering is ripe.

And the doctor gets up.

Inside the puja room the erect cow-dung *Shivalingams* cast a thousand gentle shadows upon the sparkling copper platter in which they are set out, decorated with one thousand and one white flowers and grains of rice. Amid the chanting of *mantras* and ringing of brass bells and blowing of conch shells, the good doctor and Lalita together begin to bathe the *lingams* with a constant stream of water, till all the *shlokas* are over and the benign God, with his mischevous retinue of 'Ganas': Tantra, Mantra, Ban, Ravana, Chandeesh, Bhringi and Rit, have been bidden go go back to the heavenly abode. By now the doctor doesn't know what he is thinking. He is sleepy, and there is a rich round fullness in the room with smells of incense, camphor and warm ghee. His moustache tickles.

Lalita takes three silver spoons of the amber brown holy water and drinks it down. As she gulps, the sight of her softly rippling throat pulls the doctor towards her. He can't help touching her again and again till she looks at him archly and says, 'Not here.'

'May you be blessed with a hundred sons!' says the toothless priest as he puts holy vermilion dots on their foreheads and *bilva* leaves upon their bared heads.

Within a month, they say, Aunt Lalita was pregnant with her older son, Lama, who was born a week premature but to great celebration. After eleven months, she bore her second son; and two years later, a third followed.

With this, Aunt Lalita now become Badi Amma, the Big Mother, and for the rest of her days, she was to live in her heart a great novel that she'd never write.

The Earth Goddess Transmutes

With her family complete, and the house transformed
into a fortress impregnable to all forces of disruption,
Badi Amma, once known as Lalita, who was also the
daughter of Saraswati, shook out her numerous
plumes and began to take on the contours of the
divine householder, Laxmi. For the next half-a-
century, she was to be the area's greatest stay-at-
home show-woman, a sly sorceress, who smiled in
three languages and gossiped in five.

Mostly she lay horizontal on her huge four-poster
bed, reading Sanskrit classics and reciting verses
and stories in Hindi to her offspring. She wrote to
her old teacher in Bengali and gossiped with her
husband in English. As her sharp tones began to
move like swordfish in an ocean of gritty and saline
news, the room hushed in awe. She wove Sanskrit
with Hindi and Hindi with English with the deftness
of a master weaver at his loom, handling several
shuttles at once. Words came alive at her touch,
mysterious stories took shape in intricate patterns.
As she talked, whispered and cackled, her listeners'
muscles began to twitch and their juices to flow.

Badi Amma had discovered that talked to in English, her usually monosyllabic husband revealed a similar passion for gossip. So she shrewdly surrendered to the langauge. Thus began a series of constant experiments with newer and more innovative types of verbal foreplay, as a prelude to a long and juicy horizontal life together.

'Who was that buxom woman with a deep cleavage that was constantly dropping her *pallav* in front of the deputy forest ranger at the club?' Badi Amma would ask coyly, as she moved the ochre lump of chewed pan and betel nut around her mouth with a seductive flick of a red tongue.

'Oh, she's the veterinary surgeon's youngest daughter home from convent school,' the husband would answer.

'Oh, my father!' Badi Amma would roll her eyes heavenwards, clasp her heavily beringed fingers and shake her head from side to side. The already wide nostrils of her hooked nose dilated further. 'Oh, the poor fool!'

She would then turn to her children and translate the news in Hindi,

'Isn't this the same deputy ranger sahib whose wife has run away with the grocer's son to Bombay,' one of the children would pipe in, as though on cue.

'And who was caught in a bad, bad act behind the school building,' the father would add, instead of frowning at his precocious offspring, drumming upon the lid of the silver cigarette box with his slender surgeon's fingers.

Over this strange mixture of smooth English seasoned with pungent phrases in Hindi, the family would choke and splutter with ecstasy.

The deputy ranger's pretty wife, a doe-eyed girl with a Chinese mother and an Anglo-Indian father, had married him for a love that had petered out soon after they came to live in Vishnupur. She had taken then to sleeping around with all the willing males—who were plenty—and naturally this caused talk in Vishunpur. It was not a proper way to behave in a town that had impressionable daughters and watchful mothers. Stories with moral tales had constantly to be thought up and circulated, so people would know right from wrong. That's why Badi Amma and her husband carefully nurtured the art of story-telling in their offspring, as others would teach theirs to play chess or tennis. The children were a naturally intelligent lot and their genetically sharp senses were further honed by Badi Amma's careful coaching. By the time they could speak Hindi and understand English, they'd all been turned into master story-tellers. Just as some story-tellers and writers deliberately cultivate an unprepossessing exterior to catch their prey off-guard, so also could the cherubic faces and the innocent cupid smiles of her trio of sons trick unsuspecting victims into letting their guard down.

And oh, how the grown-ups loved to talk when their hearts were full.

After each encounter worth relating, the little darlings would rush dutifully to their parents to tell them each detail before memory faded. If the scoop was too precious, they'd clap their hands to halt all conversation and gain the undivided attention of the grown-ups. This they always got.

'Raju Babu, you know . . .'

Raju Babu was the owner of a grocery shop who often travelled to a big nearby town to restock his wares. He was randy bachelor, and so a veritable cornucopia from which whole juicy bunches of fleshy lore emerged all through the year.

'Yes dear?'

'He was seen . . .'

'With some woman?'

'His own sister-in-law!'

'No!' Badi Amma would exclaim, turning to her husband with a put-on look of alarm and disbelief. 'See the *tamashas* these people put up, dear! Such *tamashas*. Such a pair, those brothers.'

'Where?' She'd turn to the little informer, the bearer of the titillating tidings.

'Where else do you think? Behind the same school building!'

Badi Amma would give a little cry of disbelief and joy, 'What a woman! To be doing it with both the brothers!'

'And God knows who else besides,' the doctor would add in a murmer designed for the children to catch.

Badi Amma would sigh with closed eyes and sway from side to side. 'No wonder her poor husband is running after any grass-cutter in skirts—and getting nicked with their sickles in the bargain.'

They'd all laugh then, uproariously and long. Afterwards, Badi Amma would order a dish of red hot chilli fritters served with a garlic chutney, and eat most of it herself.

The greatest ferreter-out of secrets and peeper-in-keyholes was the youngest son, Bittoo. Nothing was sacrosanct to his prying eyes. Like a lizard he could fit himself into any crack that looked as though it could yield secrets. By the time he was seven, he could steam open letters and pick guests' locks with bobby pins as adroitly as any professional spy. He even learnt to decipher what was written in letters already beyond his reach by holding to the mirror the blotting paper which had been used on them.

Thus the three brothers were to discover a most interesting new world through three languages, all of them laced with chillies and garlic. Their skins soaked up the words, their blood the garlic-chilli sauce. Their minds further stored away this heady mixture as a preservative for tales. Years later, in my cousin Zoomi's poetry, they were all to come tumbling out, the stories, the garlic, the chilli sauce.

♎   ♎   ♎

Since in the world of Laxmi, everything is holy: mud, dung, earth, in Badi Amma's house, the best story sessions were held in the toilet. For several years, till the boys went to boarding school, the family took at least one bowel-emptying session together. It was again at Badi Amma's behest. She said that since all diseases were first to be detected in the faeces, and since defaecating alone made people tense and lonely, and somewhat prone to constipation, why should it not be made into a happy family session, where the good doctor could, moreover, keep an informed eye on the family's stools and welfare? That's right, the indulgent husband had agreed, and added, that in his opinion, a toilet is where the body hides nothing, where all those beans and fibrous vegetables, those legumes and tiny stones from hastily swallowed berries, come tumbling out of our bodies, like long-kept secrets. The body, the children learnt, retains nothing, but nothing, beyond its needs, unless you teach it to, and then it results in nothing but rumblings and painful distensions within.

So community expulsions became the established pattern for the family through the coming years. Constipation, diarrhoea, worms, flatulence, they saw and heard each other through them all. And as time advanced, topics of conversation acquired more mature and political, even international overtones. The Profumo scandal of Britain was one such. Through detailed discussions on its various aspects, the children effortlessly picked up detailed information about, among other things, the Westminister model of government and British jurisprudence. The celebrated Nanavati affair of Bombay, where a cuckolded husband had shot dead his wife's paramour, similarly gave the brothers a comprehensive idea of how the Indian Navy is structured.

Years later, when anally-retentive covent-educated daughters-in-law, tutored by cloisters of veiled German nuns, entered this family and chanced upon references to this Neanderthal bit of togetherness, there were dark scenes between them and their husbands about the mother-in-law who wanted to initiate the next generation in the family rituals of the collective expelling of dirt.

How could she be permitted to do it to the men, generation after generation?

The alarmed daughters-in-law took to accompanying their children individually to the door of the toilet, and having secured the door from the outside, sat waiting on a chair till the lonesome brat within had dropped his load and banged on the door to be let out. Badi Amma said that the daughters-in law had been brought up unwisely and not too well. If they were, they'd not be repelled by human stools or exchanges of pleasantries between members of a family.

'A healthy scientific curiosity is what these convent-educated girls lack. It's a pity their children will be denied a chance to gain it,' the good doctor is said to have opined, and that, as they say, banged the lid down on all that.

The good doctor's own stools were precise, close-textured, well-shaped and uncoloured by fats, which he avoided almost totally in his meals. As during the family get-togethers in the bathrooms, mealtimes were for him a silent and pensive period, when he went on with his meticulously planned motions with precise and measured gestures. It was because of this, perhaps, that his frail body coped with the high altitude extremely well, in spite of the one lung left at its disposal. Badi Amma, on the other hand, loved rich, fatty foods and plenty of sweet, fleshy fruits—as did her sons. Because of this, their sittings were rather thunderous in comparison and were also interspersed with alternate bouts of constipation and flatulence.

When these happened, the doctor had a ready measure of castor oil to lubricate stopped-up guts and little brown pills to stop watery diarrhoea. Periodically, the children were also dewormed with little yellow pills. All these remedies were administered as soon as the family reassembled after the ablutions. For the washing of hands, copious use was made of red carbolic soap. Expressions of relief and happy democratic chatter were bandied about during the washing while Badi Amma and the doctor put the lids down on the commodes one by one with fond little clicks.

It was thus a healthy, happy family that Badi Amma brought up within her medical citadel in the post-Independence years, before the water scarcities began and before earthworms began to emerge from water taps. No constipation was obstinate enough, no diarrhoea too violent, no worms too recalcitrant for her husband's magic potions to cure, before the Intellectual Property Rights in the GATT Agreement complicated the medical scene. As night fell, farts resounded regularly and musically from the various bedrooms. Collective purging guaranteed that they'd be mostly without smell.

Later, when water shortages made ablutions a monitored event, and the price of anti-diarrhoea pills sky-rocketed, and the second son Zoomi became a celebrated poet and playwright, Badi Amma would wave her hand in the direction of the toilet bowl and observe that such early and fulsome blossoming of literary sensibilities was undoubtedly due to the habit of concentration he acquired in the family ritual in the toilet, in the days when both water and Intestopan were available for the asking. Later additions to the family learnt to close the doors of the loo on parents, grandparents and siblings, and thus also closed their minds to artistic sensibility, she said.

♎   ♎   ♎

The daughters-in-law cast quick and venomous glances at each other, but said nothing to their mother-in-law.

♎   ♎   ♎

Whatever the daughters-in-law may have felt, the fact was that through art and fart, a particular earthy togetherness came to bind the souls of Badi Amma's boys for life. Even after they left home with their spouses, it was this togetherness that they'd look for, and since no other house could replicate Badi Amma's, all three were to remain spiritual nomads—hard, aggressive, restless and mobile. Nothing could compensate for the loss of Badi Amma's magic citadel, with its stepped garden, the plums rotting on the ground that sent up such rich dizzyingly alcoholic vapours, and huge gourds that fattened among large, stubbled leaves like secretly pregnant women. Here, between eating and defaecation, between shadow and space, sorrow did not exist, nor time; and children were permitted to be free and forthright and to play permanently stupid games behind red curtains and green walls. When out in the garden, they were surrounded by copulating cats and gently rotting fruit. Meanwhile, the red and green house guarded them like the hood of a thousand-headed Sheshnag dozing in the sun.

Thousand-headed cobras, as Zoomi mourned again and again in his sad poems, are an extinct lot today.

$$\underline{\Omega} \quad \underline{\Omega} \quad \underline{\Omega}$$

The children came back from school at one. At precisely fifteen minutes past, their father came home from the hospital, and lunch followed. Inside, after the elaborate lunch, everyone lay on soft beds and dozed. The doctor was finicky about personal hygiene as only surgeons can be. He took all of ten minutes to wash his hands before lunch. Then, after his bath and frugal meal, he retired to his rooms to prepare for a long siesta. His movements, as he prepared for oblivion, were as beautiful and fluid as those of a dancer. With his lean and artistic fingers, he first removed his coat, with its gold stopwatch and two Parker pens. He took off the shirt and then the woollen sweater underneath. The trousers were next. When taken off they revealed striped pyjamas secured by two bicycle clips. With many clicks and snaps and metallic sounds, the doctor placed his pocketwatch, pen-knife, pens and bicycle clips upon the dresser. He was now ready to rest. Everyone wanted the father to rest, because he was so reliable, so utterly indispensable. They couldn't risk him getting fatigued and bleary-eyed.

As the good doctor slipped between the clean and sweet-smelling sheets and composed his lean limbs for slumber, everyone gently drifted into a green torpor. All but Badi Amma. She was alternately sleepy and watchful, like a giant lizard. So, in the room with dappled shadows, Badi Amma lay in bed next to her husband, carelessly exposing a good bit of one enormous and succulent, blue-veined breast. Occasionally, the doctor gently and lazily extended his hand across the gap created by the dresser. With his fingers curved in a half-moon, he held the magic rotundity for a while like Shiva's drum, the magical *dumroo*. The soft, milky mound filled his palm with plenty, and dreams with vanilla-flavoured satiation followed. Peace decended. Both husband and wife drifted into sleep within the crypt-like room with its thick, blood-coloured curtains. Wine-coloured spots of filtered light danced on the walls.

Breasts nourished the family for long.

The eldest son, Lama, was breast-fed the longest. He clung to those wonderful, pendulous bubs all through his younger brothers' infancy; past his weaning on Anna Prashan day, past Bittoo's arrival. On this hapless day, he was introduced with a bit of rice pudding to the wonderfully rich world of grains and legumes and fruits and vegetables. But nothing ever compensated for the wonderful mushroom-textured breasts that spouted for him wherever he opened his mouth to them.

Unlike his siblings, Lama cared not a bit for solid food. He curled up and buried his head in his mother's breasts like an obsessive leech, while his mouth rested on an enormous brown nipple, refusing to let go. He wanted neither cereals nor fruits. He vomited them out as soon as they were fed him He wanted only the soft nipple between his lips. They tried blending new food items, whipping them into purees, roasting, toasting or frying them. To no avail. Lama would hide his face behind his mother's *pallav*, nuzzle out the nipple in the dark, and suck

Pulled away forcibly, he went into an idiot's somnolent trance, sucking his thumb and fixing his gaze on the floor.

When he was six, the father decided to act. Badi Amma was made to put on tight brassieres with steel hooks. Ground bitter neem leaves were applied both on Lama's already misshappen thumb and the irresistably dangling breasts. When, having scratched his cheek on the offending brassiere, and successfully gotten it out of his way with his teeth, Lama put his mouth to the soft mounds, he howled. Then he spat out the green paste and put his thumb to his mouth and howled some more. He peed in his bed that night and many following nights, but the good doctor stood firm.

Finally, Lama gave up, and picked up a stutter as a lifelong punishment to his torturer.

Later, when he was to become a supporter of feminism, a bitter critic of lingerie that turned women into sex-objects, and a firm opponent of the patenting of the neem tree under the GATT agreement of the ill-famed Dunkel proposal, no one saw how he was actually avenging old unhappy battles, and his defeat of long ago.

Once Lama had been weaned, Badi Amma made sure she made him her special soft, melt-in-the-mouth rotis. These were made with flour fermented overnight with curds and soda-bicarb. She stirred crushed almonds and saffron into thickened milk that could coat the back of a wooden spoon; she also made him special Bengali sweets, flavoured with rose petals and cardamom, in a caramelised syrup.

She, the Annapurna, was not one to give up, was she?

Slowly, Lama began to eat; masticating his food listlessly and swallowing in big airy gulps that filled him up before the others could finish their meals. But Badi Amma wouldn't lose heart. Oh no. As

Lama ate, she stood by like a benevolent dragon, her fat arms folded over her ample breasts. Her expression was joyful and pious, bordering on the fanatical, much like what was to appear decades later on the hirsute faces of the *kar sevaks* that swarmed dangerously over the domes of a mosque. She made encouraging sounds and smacked her lips when urging a particularly delicious morsel into Lama's mouth. After this, all his life, Lama depended on her for taste. And it was because she was not there to urge him to eat, that Lama could fast for twenty-one days, with no discomfort, and bring down a government—and battalions of *kar sevaks* that had guarded its excesses with tridents.

We saw on television that the glass of orange juice that the party leader extended to Lama when he broke his fast had drops of what looked like mother's milk in it, gleaming like crystal ice. Lama had a gulp and bliss flooded his features. Everyone thought it was the joy of a man at the victory of his secular principles that suffused Lama's features. But we knew otherwise, and so did Badi Amma.

The Village
Goddesses

❖

Walking to school we had to cross the maidan, the only bit of flat ground in our little hill-town. A temple to the local deity of boulders, Pashan Devi, stood by the side of the narrow road that flanked the maidan. I liked going to this temple. I liked listening to the musical sound of the temple bells that resounded in the hills that formed the kingdom of the Goddess.

At the temple, hordes of men and women came and went all the time. But these were not the beautiful Shahanis, the wives of local moneylenders with enormous rings dangling from their sharp noses and their dainty wrists and ankles weighed down with family gold, who frequented the other temples of gentler, more fecund Devis. Here, in the temple of the Goddess of boulders, the fevered Matangis came. They were female sadhus with eyes reddened with hashish, carrying fearsome iron tridents with jangling bells. Drop-outs of all kinds also frequented this temple: beggars, mad men, doped-out loners and suicidal lovers. This strange congregation conversed with the Goddess as though they were her brothers and sisters. Some toothless, rheumatic old grandfathers and grandmothers also came to meet the Goddess occasionally, fumbling their way up the stairs built by one Pundit Maniram Dansila. Their arrival caused great distress to the make-shift priest who sat huddled in a narrow space. They were always knocking over his prayer books and copper pots of holy water. He really had no business to be sitting there. This Goddess of boulders needed no priestly intermediaries to reach out to her devotees. She called out to them when she wanted, and they talked back to her without fear or anger.

The Goddess heard out all calmly, promising nothing but peace. All were at home here, here where our Pashan Devi reigned, the protector of our little town and its mountains and waters. And so long as she was there, keeping vigil over the town, no major calamity could befall us, we felt.

Ω   Ω   Ω

On the outskirts of most Indian villages, in the isolation of a grove of trees, upon a hill-top, on river banks, in forests or in fields, one may find similar little structures of stone or terracotta anointed with vermilion and decorated with flowers and rice. These are votive shrine to village deities, mostly female. For the most part they are maternal and protect the villagers, but are also said to wreak havoc if angered. Lamps are lit and offerings ranging from coconuts to goats are made regularly to them as part of propitiation and appeasement rites. Clans and communities often have their own concepts of what an offering should be. The Chaudhari, Gamit and Bhil tribals of central India, for example, have offered terracotta figures to appease the Gods—a clay leg to heal a leg, a clay hand if one's own is hurt, an eye for an injured eye. For pains that are not specific or limited to one organ, symbolic offerings are made, such as a star-shaped disc for curing fainting spells and a round ball of clay for stomach-cramps. The priest transfers illnesses from humans to these objects.

If the village Goddess cannot heal, who can people say.

Down south, one such popular village deity is the fiery Mariamman. She has, it is said, a Brahmin's head and an untouchable's body. Male animals are killed to propitiate this Goddess. Far up north, in the middle Himalayan mountains, her sister Nanda, is similarly presented a male ram with four horns as sacrificial offering, amidst elaborate rituals each year.

Both these Goddesses are unmarried or have had unpleasant encounters with prospective grooms and so remained unattached. Their single status, far from making them weak and vulnerable, endows them with greater passion and power. One hears legends of certain wild celibate Goddesses who were tamed into marriage by a God—usually Shiva—who, like these Goddesses, occupies the fringes of civilization and may match them, mad act for mad act, rage for rage. Most legends, however, present the village Goddess as a passive wall that protects the villages from being decimated by the volatile male Gods. By and large, village Goddesses are a strong presence, and combine the power and passion of Kali with the grace and abundance of Laxmi.

The history of each village Goddess usually has an earthly origin. She is either the ghost of an exceptionally charismatic deceased person, or a famous queen or a local heroine who died for a cause or killed herself to prove her point. Even if a similar Goddess is to be found in another village, the first does not get universalised but remains the local deity. Most of them are harmless and symbolised by an unhewn stone that may resemble some part of the body, such as an eye or a navel. Others, the *Ugra* or violent ones, are said to manifest themselves through a human medium only at the time of ritualistic worship and are disposed of (graciously, of course), as soon as it is over.

The Children of Bormoni

Most members of the small Sar Mallo sect of Assam are fishermen by profession. Their presiding deity is Bormoni Debi. Legend has it that Bormoni was a mother who had lost nine strapping sons to the fatal lure of a mermaid who'd entice the young men when they were out fishing in the deep waters of the Brahmaputra river, make love to them and then kill them one by one with her poisonous saliva. When all her sons were dead, the grieving mother threw herself in the river, vowing to protect all the unsuspecting young fishermen of her village from the deadly enchantress. Bormoni's likeness now adorns small shrines along the river bank on crudely made altars under trees. Chanting, '*Joi Bormoni Debo*,' the men apply vermilion on the image, then on the married women and finally on their fishing nets, and place cans of fishing bait before her for her blessings. Then they all prostrate themselves before the Goddess, light camphor in small earthern saucers and place them in their boats anchored nearby. They then leave on fishing expeditions that could last several months. During this period, Bormoni Debi is their sole protector against death, temptation and several other known and unknown dangers of the deep waters. 'The Brahmaputra is our father and Boromoni Debi our mother. No one can protect us from what they cannot,' the fishermen and their women say.

Ω   Ω   Ω

The Goddesses can be both malevolent and friendly but while the benign ones are worshipped at harvest time, or at the beginning of the fishing season, special rites are conducted to appease 'wrathful' Goddesses when there is a sudden calamity like the outbreak of an epidemic or a prolonged drought, or a sudden bout of sickness among cattle or when nets and boats are damaged in inclement weather. The Goddess usually appears in the body of a woman in the village and speaks of how she has been neglected or humiliated and suggests how the villagers may now make amends for the oversight, and what sacrifices must be offered.

In Rajasthan, village Goddesses are offered, variously, vermilion, saffron, milk, yoghurt, coconut, jaggery, rice, betel-leaves and henna. Bhadana Mata of Kota, who is supposed to offer cures to victims of black magic, is offered black pulses and liquor. There are also temples to Goddesses who can cure excessive sneezing (Chink Mata in Jaipur), hiccups (Sati Mata in Fatehnagar) and sickness among cattle (Karni Mata in Bikaner, and Bhed Mata in Baseda).

The case of Shitala Mata—or mother of small pox—illustrates how the Goddess may be a life-threatening force, yet be worshipped as a saviour. The name Shitala literally means the 'cool one'. When someone is afflicted with small pox (Badi Mata) or chicken-pox (Chhoti Mata), they say he or she has been graced by the Goddess manifesting herself in his or her body, to cool off the demon, fever. All the offerings made to Shitala Mata have, therefore, cool properties, such as cold food, cool water and fans made of tender neem leaves. It is believed that this Goddess (known as Ammavaru down south) bears the onslaught of the demon, disease, and therefore must be helped, not exorcised. Her familiar is, understandably, that patient bearer of loads, the ass.

Village Goddess festivals are often the time for a voluntary inversion of normal social conduct. For example, down south, the Matangis, when possessed by the goddess Ellamma or Yellama, will break into vile abusive language, kick and push around high-caste people, drink liquor and spit it out on the onlookers, who actually feel they are being blessed by the Goddess.

The centre of Matangi worship is the village Malinthapadu, in the Kurnool district of Andhra Pradesh. A Matangi is a low-caste Madiga woman, believed to be possessed by the spirit of Mathamma. The original form of Mathamma is Yellamma. Often, a Matangi will break into wild songs, glorying in the abuse of proud high-caste folk, whose homes she then visits, smears their pots with cow-dung, and demands gifts of them. Food, bodices from women in the family, even headscarves and sacred threads from the males, are given her. Then she leaves, still abusing them and spewing toddy on their bodies. Everyone is happy at this degradation, which is believed to bring good luck.

The Matangi's wild abandon is taken to be a manifestation of the Goddess's chaotic powers. It is surrender to a phenomenon that is beyond logic and order, and is therefore cathartic of the suddenness and despair with which chaos strikes human lives and society. To worship Goddesses such as Manasa, the goddess of snakes, Shitala, the Goddess of small pox and Shashthi, of infant death, is to realise simultaneously the frailty of life, and the extent to which protection may be available for the faithful.

My Cousin's Eyes

'Children,' said Mother to us, 'close your eyes and go to sleep.' From the adjoining room where the elders sat, we could hear voices. My aunt was crying. The doctor had confirmed their worst fears. Her eldest had a rare disease of the cornea. He would lose his sight in a year's time, if nothing was done about it.

A chill wind was blowing outside. Our eyes stung. Our brilliant cousin had wanted to be a surgeon. It was a very unpleasant sound to hear elders' voices breaking, followed by silence. It made one shiver.

We learnt later that the family had pooled in their resources to arrange for a corneal transplant for our cousin. The women had sworn to present the goddess Naina Devi with a pair of gold eyes should the boy regain his sight. The cousin left for England. One aunt kept vigil. She sat at the table and waited for the postman. The silence in her house, which used to be full of the boisterous laughter of boys, rang in our ears. When the phone rang, the parents went pale. Everyone prayed. We visited the temple everyday, and hoped, and prayed some more.

My cousin's operation was a success. Everyone said it was by the grace of the Goddess.

$$\Omega \qquad \Omega \qquad \Omega$$

Again somewhere between sleep and awakening we heard someone tell someone else how the aunt was desperate because her mother-in-law had refused to part with even an ounce of the family gold needed to fashion the promised pair of golden eyes for the Goddess. She felt it unnecessary after all the medical expenses they had incurred. Money didn't grow on trees, she said.

'Mothers-in-law!' someone said, and sighed, as though that explained it all.

The aunt, we learnt later, kept her promise to the Goddess by selling her gold bangles. The mother-in-law died a few years later, leaving her a trunk full of gold. If her own daughters-in-law are to be believed, the aunt now hoards it just as tightly.

♎   ♎   ♎

Daughters-in-law!

The Hungry Daughter-in-law

Once there was this woman who had a real shrew for a mother-in-law. Since the daughter-in-law worked very hard and loved good food, the old woman saw to it that she was kept busy with various chores outside her kitchen and got little of the food and none of the real delicacies she had cooked for the family. As a result, the daughter-in-law was said to have been starving. Once, the mother-in-law cooked a most delicious dish of bitter gourds. The fact that her daughter-in-law loved bitter gourds was good enough reason for her to serve her only some boiled rice, with a pinch of salt and one green chilli. Then she sent her off to fill the water pots from the river. When the mother-in-law's back was turned, the meek daughter-in-law did the unthinkable. She stole some curry and rice, and hid it inside her empty water pot before she left to fetch the water.

On the lonely banks of the village river, there

stood this temple of the village Goddess. The daughter-in-law stole in, bolted the door, sat down in front of the idol and happily ate the rice and curry. The sight shocked the Goddess so much that, as she watched the daughter-in-law bolt down her food, she cupped her chin in wonder in her palm, and stayed that way.

The daughter-in-law didn't notice all this. Having made a hearty meal of the stolen rice and curry, she went out and rinsed first her mouth and then her pot. She then filled the pot with fresh water and went home. Soon after this, when the village priest happened to go into the temple, he was aghast to find the Goddess holding her chin in her hand instead of extending it in the traditional gesture of benediction to the villagers. The priest ran out screaming that the Goddess was angry and considering retribution. The villagers agreed it was indeed a bad omen. Some said the new posture foreshadowed a drought, others, an epidemic. Still others predicted an attack on the village by dacoits or a band of murderous demons. Who could tell what would not happen when the Goddess altered her stance? Soon the whole village was trembling and the men sat till late in the village square, smoking their hookahs and working out elaborate rituals to appease the angry Goddess. The food in village kitchens went cold since the women could not eat till the men had eaten, no matter how hungry they were.

The poor daughter-in-law had had a long day and was longing to eat whatever food was left for her and then go to sleep. Then she found that all the curious elderly women had gone off to the village square to hear what was being debated there. While the elders debated the issue, the hungry daughter-in-law stole to the temple. Once inside the temple, she locked the door and faced the Goddess, arms akimbo.

In angry tones she began to quarrel with her. 'Who do you think you are? Were you never a wife and a daughter-in-law? Do you not know how many ruses a daughter-in-law must employ in order to survive in her mother-in-law's house, till she becomes a mother-in-law herself? What kind of a woman are you, pretending to be shocked that I stole in and ate a bit of curry and rice in front of you? Have you no shame! Put your hand down now, or I'll hit you on the head with my pot.'

Slowly, they say, the Goddess repaired to her earlier posture, looking serene and benevolent once more. The daughter-in-law now rushed to the square to tell everyone that the statue was as it always was, and that the old priest must have been hallucinating, inhaling all those fumes from the incense in the temple.

♎   ♎   ♎

Stories such as the one above were lived through or crafted together by an unknown woman heaven knows how many centuries ago. But they can still come. through to us alive and crackling. The inexorability of religious laws, the inevitabiliity of the mother-in-law's dominance and the desire to defy both till one's own time comes—none of these has changed for most Indian women. The listeners to the story in my mother's generation would perhaps laugh and praise the young woman's cleverness and modesty in keeping both her defiance of oppression and her successful challenge to the Goddess a secret from the village. They would identify with her, as someone who survived an unjust and unfair system with cleverness, good humour and modesty. But many in my generation, and most in my daughters' would not see her as a rebel at all, but as a sad example of a fiery spirit curbed by the dead weight of a patriarchal power-paradigm. To them, the Goddess expressing surprise over a daughter-in-law's daring instead of striking the wicked mother-in-law dead, would be sound proof of religion being women's enemy, even when it was a Goddess who presided over the human scene.

The difference between the two reactions is not related as much to a decline in religious faith among the educated urban young, as to a basic change in the way we today approach the enigma of the Devi.

For the original listeners and makers-up of such legends, there lay beyond the temporal life of the hapless daughters and daughter-in-law, a timeless domain where femaleness transcended both life and divinity. Where being born a girl, a *kanya*, made you a Goddess. The daughter-in-law, as a woman, would share this *kanya*-hood with the village Goddess as easily as she shared a sari or a pod of tamarind or a flower garland with her sisters, often with some gentle banter and good-natured grumbling. It was such a mutual bond that the hungry daughter-in-law invoked when she shouted the Goddess out of her catatonic stillness.

For those who do not have memories of mothers and grandmothers laughing, weeping, and talking to statues in temples, nor of been feted as little Goddesses during their pre-pubescent years, there is perhaps no room for such happy affinity with the Goddesses. This impasse in the heart of the modern Indian woman is a reflection of our times. So much of our imagination is dominated by the current politics of state that we have given literature and lore largely the go-by. And yet, in ignoring story and legend, we deprive ourselves of history.

Ω   Ω   Ω

Here is a story. It happened a long time ago, in the small hill town that I came from. It is all about loving intensely, jealously guarding one's love and aggressively striving to grab at it, even in the face of death.

There was this plain-looking girl, who was a childhood friend of my mother's elder sister. She was said to have fallen deeply in love with a handsome young man who was already engaged to be married to a young girl, tales of whose beauty were legion. It was, as the Americans might say, a no-win situation. My aunt, having failed to pull her friend out of her great crush, advised her to appeal to the Goddess at the Tripura Sundari temple. Each morning thereafter, this lovelorn maiden would go and light a lamp with pure ghee at the Devi's temple, and invoke her powers, so she could marry her young man. She continued this even after the young man got married to his lovely lady. The plain one gave an ultimatum to the Goddess that she had to sort out things for her devotee, or the latter would personally break the noses of the two stone lions flanking the temple doors, come the next Navratri. It was said that, soon after this, news came that the beauteous one had died suddenly, leaving the field clear for my aunt's plain friend.

She was, my aunt said, in due course married to her young man and together they went on to parent many children and lived happily ever after.

The Dark Shaktis

The story of the evolution of the aggressive manifestations of the Goddess goes back to Sati's great confrontation with her father Daksha, over the non-inclusion of Sati's spouse Shiva in the list of invitees to the great fire sacrifice. It is said that when hot-headed Sati was unable to persuade Shiva to give her permission to go, she began multiplying herself and out of these manifestations of her divine wrath came the ten *Mahavidyas*: Kali, Tara. Chhinnamasta, Bhuvaneswari, Bagala, Dhoomavati, Kamala, Matangi, Shodashi and Bhairavi.

In the Shakta tradition, these *Mahavidyas* or revelations, correspond to the Vaishnava concept of the ten avatars of Vishnu. The *Guhyatiguhya Tantra* indeed gives a list of the ten *Mahavidyas* and goes on to establish that each avatar of Vishnu actually arose out of a particular *Mahavidya*.

Anyway, born out of a hot-blooded woman's anger, these Goddesses are uniformly worshipped as fearsome warrior deities. According to the *Kalika Purana*, Kali is naked and holds a severed head and a bloodied cleaver, while Bhairavi's breasts are smeared with blood and her eyes are always rolling in her head in a drunken stupor. Chhinnamasta stands in a cremation ground atop the copulating bodies of Kama (the God of love) and his wife Rati, (some legends say it is Krishna and Radha). Tara is similarly dark, rests her left foot on a corpse, wears a necklace of severed heads and laughs a most horrible laugh. Bagala has the head of a crane, and is depicted beating an enemy with a club in one hand while pulling out his tongue with the other. Dhoomawati is a mournful, toothless widow. Tall, stern, and unsmiling, she dresses in dirty clothes and her withered breasts hang to her navel. She is said to be querulous and rides a crow. The seventh, Matangi, is fat, dark, ugly and always drunk.

In contrast to these are the three benign *Matrikas*: Shodashi, a sixteen-year-old with a flushed face. She has intercourse with Shiva while stretched out over a pedestal formed by the bodies of Brahma and Vishnu. Others are the ever-smiling Bhuvaneshwari, and Kamala, who stands on a lotus.

It is said that the primary function of these ten Goddesses was to frighten Shiva into granting permission to Sati to visit her father. As Sati, the Goddess was a meek and obedient Hindu wife, but she contained fearsome independent spirits within which overwhelmed anyone who dared oppose her. In both the *Brahaddharma Purana* and *Mahabbhagavata Purana*, the Devi says that these fierce manifestations are generated periodically by her so that through them her devotees may acquire special powers over their enemies such as the forces that cause emotional disturbances, neurological disorders, slackness or confusion of the mind.

The juxtaposition of the auspicious with the inauspicious, as these Goddesses portray, is not mere aberration. It is, in fact, a central feature of all Goddess-lore. Since the need for nourishment must coexist with the need for creation, giving with being given, awesome creativity must therefore go hand in hand with an awesome hunger for life's blood. With their killing and drinking of blood, the Goddesses continually recycle life and death on earth.

There are other roving bands of divine mothers, such as the sixteen *Matrikas* of the Shakta pantheon. At the bottom of the hand-painted icons of the three great goddesses, these *Matrikas* always appear as sixteen abstract signs.

The *Vana Parva* in the *Mahabharata* also mentions a group of six childless killer females, sent by the jealous God Indra, to kill Kartikeya, a divine warrior born of Shiva's burning hot semen after the river Ganga had patiently taken it in and cooled it with her icy waters. As the would-be murderesses approached the superbly lovely child, however, maternal love overtook them. They forgot their instructions and their breasts began to ooze milk. They then gave the child suck and cared for him till he grew into manhood.

Another story depicts these Goddesses as six powers of the divine child, Kartikeya, which would grow in number and present themselves in the form of sixteen militant female deities who protected him when Indra tried to strike him with his thunderbolt, Vajra.

There is yet another story that makes the *Matrikas* the wronged and vengeful wives of six sages, charged by their husbands with adultery. Whether they were bribed by Indra into becoming killers, or forced by uncaring and unfair husbands into this state, the *Matrikas* are generally perceived to be a band of unhappy, unfulfilled, childless women who are powerful nevertheless, and have a special penchant for afflicting infants. Association with Kartikeya and, later, with Buddha, is said to have transformed them somewhat, and made them more benign, but they did not undergo a radical change of heart even then, and are shown reverting again and again into raging infernos of murderous revenge.

The Sad Tale of Saruli and Hiraballabh

It was on the way back from the Vishnupur Civil Hospital that Hiraballabh, the compunder, was said to have chanced on a glimpse of Saruli collecting the laundry from the bushes surrounding Badi Amma's house. A tall girl with a full figure, she was of a wheatish complexion, with large doe-like eyes. 'The dart of Kamdeva,' a breathless Zoomi told the family within five minutes of this encounter, 'has struck our Hiraballabh Babu!'

Saruli was born twenty years prior to this encounter, in a tiny straw-lined room in the nearby prostitutes' village, Naikyana. She was the daughter of an unknown father and Pusuli, an aging harlot from Rampur, come up to Naikyana to die. The pregnant woman had, they say, fallen on bad times. She had known, moreover, that the world beyond this village did not welcome children of the poor, least of all the daughter of a down-at-heel prostitute, and so had tried to abort the foetus with horrible-tasting broths made of herbs and spices, hot compresses, long treks up and down the mountains, and even the butt of a sickle. But Saruli, even as an embryo, had clung to the walls of her mother's woman with the tenacity that was later to characterize her life.

The mother's lack of affection shall, Badi Amma said, always touch the soul of the unborn child, and so, she said, Saruli was born with the soul of a dented grinding-stone. Hira, the midwife, alone disagreed. Although she had delivered hundreds of other prostitutes' babies, she loved Saruli with a deep and unpretentious love, almost as though she had borne her in her own womb.

As Saruli emerged screaming and writhing, all covered in crimson blood and after-birth, Hira had hung her upside down like a skinned rabbit and,

screwing up her wise eyes against the gloom,
pronounced happily, 'Well, praise be to the Goddess,
it is a pretty girl such as I have never seen in this
village. She'll bring the family loads of silver, that's
for sure.'

In later life, the toothless midwife's love was to
protect Saruli against much, including her mother's
wrath whenever the urge to beat the daylights out of
her pig-headed, precocious and stony-hearted
daughter overtook Pusuli. Saruli was a perfect
coquette by the time she was ten, and everyone who
looked her in the eye knew that this child would not
stay on the straight and narrow. Things awaited her
even outside the confines of the little village of
Naikyana, whether Pusuli liked it or not.

Badi Amma said she had happened to see Saruli
bathing naked in the stream in the forest near
Vishnupur where she had gone out to paint. She
asked Saruli if she might like to come away to
Vishnupur with her and maybe even go to school.
'Go, child, go!' urged her toothless mentor Hira,
with tears streaming down her walnut cheeks.
'Memsahib will make a *mem* out of you. Your mother
will not live too long, anyway.' Everyone in the
village, including Hira, felt that after this encounter
with the doctor's wife, Saruli's life would achieve
some direction. Saruli is said to have snorted and
said, 'So let her die! I am off,' though no one would
know which way and to what end, for a long, long
time to come. That is what *Karma's* ways are all
about, Badi Amma said.

☊   ☊   ☊

'What a shining roof and what a huge house!'
These were the first words Saruli uttered when

she stood overawed in front of Badi Amma's house. She had left her mother quite happily, further confirming to the villagers their earlier pronouncements about her established wayward nature. The old midwife was in the grip of tuberculosis by now, and the same disease had overtaken Pusuli, whom the good doctor declared to be beyond treatment. He referred her to a sanatorium nearby, run by one of his old friends. This assured her two meals a day, a real mattress under her and real blankets to cover her shame. This was the last Saruli saw of her mother. No tears were shed at the parting, on either side.

When news of Saruli's arrival reached the kitchen quarters, Zoomi wrote us, Badi Amma's band of devoted retainers went into a tizzy. Daulat, the hashish-smoking Brahmin eccentric, in charge of the kitchen and the Gods, started banging the lids on the pots and roaring out dire warnings about how a harlot's arrival at an august house could result in nothing but trouble and more trouble. He had to be shut up with a mug of chilled water thrown at him by the cheeky scrubber of pots, Bhuniya, the low-caste, at Lama and Zoomi's suggestion.

Ω   Ω   Ω

'Let me take you to the kitchen,' said Badi Amma to Saruli when the boys eventually reported peace in the kitchen quarters. Saruli allowed herself to be led quite happily.

The three brothers were in the kitchen quarters sooner than the mother and the maid. They watched with concealed glee as Daulat turned purple. 'You'll have to kill me before the polluted harlot's feet cross my threshold,' said Daulat, leaping out of the kitchen and swaying slightly, looking, for all the world, Zoomi said, like a caricature of the celibate monkey god Hanuman. Daulat was a purity freak. On her unclean days even Badi Amma was forbidden to step into his domain.

Saruli giggled, swaying her hips and rolling her eyes. 'I shall not enter your kitchen, Guru Maharaj,' she said. 'I am but a mere woman. I shall quietly wash clothes out there in the courtyard for the *sahib* and the *mem*. Just give me a bucket of water, a brass mug, a cake of detergent soap and a wooden mallet and you'll see me no more.' So saying, she removed her shawl and at this they saw the fair round arms that emerged from her ugly blouse like the stems of twin lotus flowers.

There was a general catching of breath amongst the crowd. The brothers even heard a voice compare her breasts to twin Himalayan peaks.

All this silenced Daulat, who retreated, like the defeated simian king Bali, into the smoke-filled netherworld he had emerged from, muttering and growling.

After that, Saruli was always happy. She brought much cheer to everyone and all the servants were glad of her presence. Of the general favours she distributed with such love, they never talked.

All this, till Hiraballabh entered the scene, carrying a box of gauze and squealing like a pig because Parabhoo the drunkard had given him a sudden fright near the gate.

Trained by an Englishman, this gifted low-caste cook, Parabhoo, was thrown out of the kitchens of the local club for having burnt the Christmas cake after a drunken orgy. Earlier in the day, as Bittoo was to inform Hiraballabh, Parabhoo had consumed two bottles of home-brewed *malta* liquor and had since been singing elegies to his late mother, sitting on a pear tree. The sight of poor Hiraballabh had suddenly provoked him into clambering down the tree with a furious bellow.

Had Parabhoo not startled Hiraballabh into hysterical screaming, perhaps Saruli would not have rushed to the scene like a half-naked nymph and the compounder would have quietly gone in, left his box in the pantry, and after his customary glass of smoky tea with the servants, gone off to play football as usual.

But the movements of one's *Karma*, as the blind sage had said, Badi Amma reflected, cannot be changed.

♎   ♎   ♎

It was a morning soon after a most glorious spring had set ablaze the rhododendrons on the hillside next to our house, and the pear tree was in bloom. Hiraballabh had come to his boss' house with a box of sterilized gauze that Badi Amma had needed for straining jellies with. At that point, Saruli, with her golden arms exposed to the sun, chose to gather the washing from the backyard, singing lustily of her love for a man with a black cap worn askew.

Inside the kitchen, Daulat ('Just picture it,' Zoomi said to us) was cursing this springtime effervescence of the accursed whore, hitting various pots with his iron ladle like Javanese gongs.

'Just picture it,' Zoomi had said.

It was worth picturing.

The curses of the cantankerous celibate pierced through the smoke-filled kitchen air like knives. Salt spilled, turmeric flew and chillies lay spluttering in mustard oil. All this was designed by Daulat to force the vile phlegm from lust-filled throats.

At the vision of such beauty, against the strange

smells and sounds that wafted around her, Hiraballabh forgot his hysterical screeching and also what his errand was. He even lost his tongue, as he chanced upon this singing beauty with two pajamas on her left shoulder and four of Badi Amma's enormous brassieres dangling from her fingers. All he could say was—'*Hai!*'

A small crowd of servants and children collected around the two. Saruli first winked at the audience and then, with a tinkling laugh, gently swung the brassieres at the turned-to-stone compounder, whereupon one of the hooks got caught in the hapless man's pocket. Thus, it was like a bewildered puppy on a lead that Saruli playfully marched a literally hooked lover-to-be into the curtained and red interiors of the house.

Badi Amma, who was embroidering a handkerchief, looked up as they entered.

'Such a thing never grew in Lord Indra's gardens,' Saruli is said to have declared to her mistress, doubling over in mirth as she presented Hiraballabh to her.

'Indeed it did not, you silly girl!' Badi Amma said in a not entirely admonishing tone to Saruli. 'Let the poor man off and fold those clothes.' Then she turned to Hiraballabh. 'Yes, Hirua, what have you brought in that box under your arm?'

Hiraballabh snapped out of his daze and began to undo the string around the cardboard box with trembling fingers. He could not, however, collect his wits sufficiently to tell the mistress what was in it. The crowd that had followed him in roared and nudged each other and demanded to know what the gauze was for, while Saruli nuzzled close to him, pretending to unhook him but getting him more and more entangled.

'Shame on you, Hirua, you a married man and father of four? She'll break your heart, do you hear?' Badi Amma said. 'Don't forget she is a Naik girl who'll first make you love her and then ruin you. There are many before you that've chased these Naik skirts, only to be kicked in the face afterwards.'

The roomful of people almost choked, laughing at the hapless idiot who couldn't see anything beyond Saruli's cleavage. Had he been able to, perhaps he would have changed his sad fate, but as everyone knows, fate is to man what a flame is to a moth. If there was no fate, there would be no stories, no songs, no flames, no charred wings.

Saruli finally detached the gigantic bras from Hiraballabh, then sailed off into the garden declaring her intention of fetching more laundry, and having deposited the box, Hiraballabh too walked out after her, a doomed, dazed, if somewhat fat, moth.

At this point, Badi Amma's boys, Lama and Zoomi, made themselves invisible, following the lovers-to-be, secretly melting into the shadows that dappled the huge garden that was singing and sighing with birds and bees. They reported later to us that once outside, Saruli had begun to sing her lusty love couplets once again. Her voice was as clear as a bell and singing was her greatest pleasure. She did not, however, restrict herself to devotional songs in temples like other young women in the town did. When she sang, she did so outside in the open, while bathing in a spring or putting out laundry to dry in Badi Amma's garden. She created her own verses as she went along and added to them names of people that she knew, the way one strings together a long chain of wild flowers for the Gods.

Today, she sang of a certain Hirua and Saruli, who were caught in a whirlpool like two pine logs that were destined to be separated at the end of their journey by river, who were made for each other just like fragrant tea and a gleaming brass tumbler, or a gold nose-ring and the pair of lips it dangles over.

For weeks, thereafter, Hirua and Saruli, Zoomi said, went swimming in a torrential river of love that was said to have been full of many eddies and whirlpools. Like two logs swimming side by side, for some time, they were inseparable.

Saruli put on her best ornaments while on this voyage. They comprised many strings of beads, safety-pins and coins, and as the couple lay on rocks near the ridge, she told Hiraballabh tales of her village. About how all the great and mighty ones of seventy-five villages around hers dropped by at Naikyana for such great and glorious voyages of discovery as theirs promised to be. How women in her village knew the ways of men from Kali Kumaon, across the Kali river, down to the plains of Bareilly and Rampur. All the big shop-owners and landlords, the poets and the singers, the students and the teachers, wanted to go on such voyages. Who was he to refuse?

Then the fall came.

As Badi Amma had predicted, Saruli began to see someone else, the dandy Mahesh Babu.

Lama-Zoomi's eight-page letter in green ink described to us, in minute detail, the end when it came. It seems that the abandoned Hiraballabh, unable to retrace his way to the mother of his four children, or find escape in drink like his predecessors had, went and hanged himself from the ceiling of his room and died a most hideous death, just two days after the Vishnupur team won the football match against the Ranikhet boys.

When the police cut the rope and brought the body down, the letter reported, several sigh-like sounds escaped from the body. Badi Amma said they were love words, suppressed inside the poor suffocated breast of the dead compunder; but the good doctor thought they were just gases. He should've known, the boys wrote, since he did the autopsy and found that the poor man had venereal disease as well.

The doctor now prevailed on Badi Amma to discharge Saruli from service as soon as her course of antibiotics was over. The doctor also informed the family in the toilet that the term 'post-mortem' is British, that the Americans prefer to use the older Latin word, 'autopsy'. He carefully spell it out for them—a-u-t-o-p-s-y.

'What does it mean?' Lama asked, his voice high and surprisingly close to tears.

'It means seeing for yourself, because during the days of the Romans, bodies of all those who died a violent and unnatural death were displayed for people to see and verify the manner of death for themselves.'

'That was sensible,' muttered Badi Amma, beginning to wash herself.

During the collective hand-washing with Lifebuoy soap, the doctor also told them how perfect the heart, the kidneys and the liver were within the corpse of Hiraballabh. 'He was good for another fifty years, at least,' he said, wiping his delicate surgeon's fingers carefully, one by one, on the Turkish hand towel.

'The man was murdered by his heart,' Badi Amma said firmly. 'You can cut and lay bare everything, but you'll never know what the heart was thinking, when he died,' she said.

No more was said on the subject.

Ω   Ω   Ω

During Saruli's treatment for VD, the boys wrote, she had stayed in a small room on the outskirts of the town, with no one to sit with her. For some days, the people at the house slept badly.

After her cure, Saruli disappeared, no one knew where.

♎   ♎   ♎

Years later, during one of his visits, Lama said he saw her with a white sadhu at a railway station in Prayag. She wore saffron, he said, but her eyes held no renunciation. Lama also said that he strained his eyes to follow her but she was gone. A few days later, newspapers were rife with reports about the most abominable murder of a very mysterious and very rich white guru at an exclusive hill resort. It was hinted that the guru's companion, one Saruli Devi, had decamped with the late guru's priceless collection of gems and antiques.

Badi Amma had taken one look at the photographs and said, 'That's her, that's Saru.' And the name was one that the hapless Hiraballabh had given her in a moment of love.

But by then Badi Amma's eyesight was beginning to cloud over with milky cataracts and her memory with Alzheimer's disease, so one could be sure.

Still, one often wondered about it all . . .

The Five Memorable Ones

'*Ahilya, Draupadi, Tara, Kunti, Mandodari tatha.
Panch kanya smarennityam mahapataknshanam.*'

The elders, shaking droplets of cold water from
their spare Brahmin forms, chanted these lines each
morning. We were told that recounting the names of
the *panch kanyas*—Ahilya, Draupadi, Tara, Kunti
and Mandodari (five heroines from the epics
Ramayana and *Mahabharata*) every morning would
atone for even the most heinous of sins.

In common usage today, the word *kanya* has came
to mean a virgin. In the *Mahabharata*, however, the
sun God tells Kunti that the root word of this word
is *kam*—to desire—thus *kanya* means one who is
free to desire anyone, anytime. This interpretation
somehow fits in with these memorable women.
Ahilya, Draupadi, Tara, Kunti and Mandodari were
five extraordinarily talented women, grossly
mistreated by their men. They chose, however, not
to walk out on their bad marriages but to reassert
their right to stand on the side of truth and justice.
All five ultimately won the right to a fair hearing

from history and were reinstated in their former glory.

Throughout their lives, though, they stood alone on the side of truth. Alone and suffering.

Austere, brooding, insatiate, truth—these tales reveal—is a terrible master.

☊   ☊   ☊

Stories crowd around such lives naturally and effortlessly. There is something for everyone in here: grandeur, treachery and duplicity, the rape of individuality, and the creation of kings and parliaments and posterity. The majority of the male and female contemporaries of these tragic women, though, just stand around them, watching their suffering as passive spectators. If they are worried or sorry, it is mostly not for these women, but for themselves. Their sheepish instinct for self-preservation and a certain petulant envy prevent them from understanding fully what these women are all about.

Only the poets are capable of doing that.

Valmiki and Vyasa, two poets who wrote about these women, themselves stood on the edge of society. As refugees fleeing their people and their times, these poet-saints have wrested for the women the right to be heard by history.

The poets' empathy with the five *kanyas* is really rooted in the fact of their own wayward lives. Valmiki was a murderous dacoit whose life turned around completely at the sight of a hunter's arrow piercing a pair of copulating *krauncha* birds. Suddenly, they say, he burst into a genre of poetry that was startlingly different from that of the classics:

Ma Nishad, pratishtha twamgamah shashwati sama.

'Oh thou Nishad (Heartless One), may you not win renown for hundreds of years.'

The dark and ugly Vyasa, the creator of the *Mahabharata*, was another social dropout. He, the illegitimate son of queen Satyavati, had chosen to live in self-imposed exile on a little island between two rivers and came to be known as Krishna Dwaipayana Vyasa. When his half-brother, the king Vichitravirya, died suddenly, he was asked by Vichitravirya's step-brother, Bhishma, to sire sons to protect the royal line, since Bhishma was himself sworn to celibacy. The recently widowed young queens of Vichitravirya recoiled from a revolting intimacy with a stranger with matted hair, and calloused, rough hands, but when forced to lie with him, one bound her eyes with a scarf and the other smeared her body with mud. The ugly stranger obliged each queen out of a sense of duty—beneath which, one is sure, lay a deep sense of sadness and shame. The results of these couplings were freaks: one baby born blind, the other frail and riddled with jaundice. Sired in loathing and conceived in sorrow, together these two princes and their legitimate and illegitimate sons went on to trigger off one of the bloodiest civil wars in legend—the Mahabharata. A war with which the earth, as the poet Vyasa said to his mother, would lose her youth, and the day its innocence.

Vyasa, a sad witness to the end of an era that he had unwillingly helped perpetrate, sent his ageing mother off to the forests as the fratricidal war began, and himself left for his dark island.

Vyasa and Valmiki alone could have recaptured

for posterity the lives and the strange times of these five memorable women who turned to the truth and burned as a consequence.

Turned and burned.

Some burned and some were to go on and on, even as the earth lost its youth and the day its innocence.

Ahilya

Ahilya appears in the *Ramayana*, a strangely nondescript ('*hala*' means 'ugly') wife, always prepared to retreat. She was ascetic power incarnate, always walking soft-footed, diffidently and with some embarrassment behind her sage husband, Gautama. The simple Ahilya was tricked by that lecherous and deceitful Lord of the Gods, Indra, into sleeping with him. She genuinely believed that the imposter posing as her husband was indeed he, the sage Gautama. She told her husband so when he came back from his bath at the river bank and saw her in Indra's arms. Indra's womanising and powers of impersonation were well-known. But the rishi, in the manner of all righteous men, was short of temper and hard of hearing. So he cupped holy water in his palm and cursed his innocent wife. Ahilya turned into a grey boulder and it would be ages before the touch of Lord Rama's feet broke the spell and she became a *kanya* again. It was obvious to Rama as she took shape that here was an extraordinary woman. Valmiki describes the grand aura Ahilya wore as she re-emerged. So moved was Ram by the sight, that he touched her feet and asked his younger brother to do likewise. 'Such grace must be bowed to,' Vyasa says.

Ahilya blessed Ram and his brother graciously. She was as free of taint as she was of rancour.

♎   ♎   ♎

'*Hala*' means 'ugly'.

In the language of the tribe of the Nankani, in north of Lebanon, the word for ugly and free, they say, is the same.

♎   ♎   ♎

September 1992: Bhanvari Bai is a dark, tall and thin woman with a straight carriage and sad eyes peering out of a prematurely aged face. There is nothing obviously heroic or beautiful about her. She is the humble village potter's wife and was working as a village-level social worker, a 'Sathin', under a Rajasthan state government-run developmental project. One of her given duties was to prevent the practice of retrograde social customs such as the illegal child-marriages that were rampant in her area. When she tried to stop one of these, a powerful lobby of village males is alleged to have attacked her family, broken the pots they had baked for sale and dragged Bhanwari out of her hut. Then the men gang-raped her. While she was being raped, her flailing husband was held down by the men and made to watch her humiliation before being beaten unconscious himself, she reported to the police.

After this, the village ostracised Bhanwari and her children.

Since the police were reluctant to act, Bhanwari's case was taken up by various women's groups.

Petitions were filed. Caste ties are strong in the villages, and since all of Bhanwari's alleged rapists were from the dominant castes, it took several women's groups to get the crime registered. Even after this, the guilty were allowed to escape the police dragnet for months. Bhanwari and the women then petitioned the state High Court and after considerable dragging of feet, the guilty were apprehended. Meanwhile, word had spread. Bhanwari was given an award for exceptional bravery. Then another followed. The weary village was shaken out of its resignation. People began to talk to her and her family once again.

Slowly, life began to assume normalcy for Bhanwari and her family.

Then, one day, the state government decided that it must terminate the services of Bhanwari and all other women village-workers and close down the women's development programme that had employed them. They had no funds, the ruling party said. A few years before, before their party swung into power, the same political group of men had supported a case of sati, where a young woman had been forced to die on her husband's pyre. It is an honourable woman's *dharma* to commit sati, their leader had said, as they cracked coconuts at the revered spot and bowed low in respect to the dead woman, by now deemed a Goddess.

Regardless of protests, to which they were accustomed, the bureaucracy and the political parties chose, in the meanwhile, to dispense fat grants-in-aid to countless other non-governmental projects. These projects would eventually be headed by ex-politicians and ex-bureaucrats who could tabulate areas for improvement and submit their project papers in triplicate within two days, before the expiry of the financial year. How could the illiterate 'Sathins' match their sagacity and competence?

Thus are injustices perpetrated in contracts and coconuts.

Ω   Ω   Ω

Bhanwari, however, is not one to give up. She believes she has many female supporters. Out of the award-money she has collected, she wants to spend twenty-five thousand rupees on repairing a pond in her desert village, so the cattle would have enough drinking water. With another twenty-five thousand rupees, she wishes to start a trust which will give awards to women like her.

She is working again at preventing child-marriages and, asked about the future, she says she'll think about it. 'I'm not alone now, that much I know,' she asserts.

She says this again when a Sessions Court sets her alleged rapists free, and thousands of women march in the streets all over India in protest.

'I am not alone now. That much I know.'

As she says this, her dark weather-beaten face is set hard as a stone.

Hala may mean ugly, but it also means free.

Ω   Ω   Ω

Then there is Repe Murmu, a tribal woman from West Bengal. She was married to a drunkard in 1986. Within six months of marriage her husband had begun ill-treating her and Repe had ultimately to run away from home to save her life. She approached the all-woman village panchayat for justice. The members forced Repe's husband to take her back. Since then, Repe has been instrumental in the reunion of ten estranged couples in the area. Repe's husband, Bhola, is a chastened man today and has stopped drinking. The women of the area, encouraged by their success, and just as tired of their drunken, lazy and promiscuous males, have ransacked all the shops that sold illicitly-brewed liquor and even destroyed the works where it was distilled. Today, in the Keshiary area of Midnapur district, the men have got a clear message: Quit drinking. Take back your wives. Or face the consequences.

Such grace, as Valmiki said, must be bowed to.

Ω   Ω   Ω

July 1995: The Usha Multi-Purpose Cooperative Stores in Calcutta is a body with a membership of six hundred prostitutes. With a deposit of seven thousand rupees collected from fifty members, the society came into being on June 22, 1995. The membership of the society, its papers state, 'is open to female individuals above the age of eighteen, including sex-workers and ex-sex workers, as well as sympathisers'.

According to one member, Sadhana Mukherjee, a prostitute herself, some legal difficulties cropped up when the idea was first mooted. The laws relating to the formation of a cooperative laid down that its members would have to be of good moral character.

Morality? That is a secondary consideration when human lives are at stake, said the members angrily.

Among women engaged in a profession where one is paid on a per-day, per-customer basis, where availability through the day and night is everything and profits only for the pimps, anger collects like lethal sewer gases, and ignites with the smallest spark.

To the unknowing, however, the women look like blocks of grey stone, dozing on the doorsteps of the brothels in daytime, awaiting release.

Morality? They laugh, and spit in the open drains. They are *hala*, they are free.

Hala in Sanskrit also means 'girlfriend'.

Draupadi

It was a fire of revenge against his enemies that her father Drupad had lit. The dusky Draupadi arose from the flames, arrogantly beautiful, luminous and calm. Along with her brother Drishtidyumua and the hermaphrodite Shikhandi, she was to make up a major force in the great civil war of the *Mahabharata*, in which her father, King Drupad's enemies were to be decimated, besides much else.

Much has been written about how this rare woman was won by Kunti's favourite son, the Pandava, Arjuna, in an archery contest. And how an absentminded instruction by Kunti led to Draupadi being shared as a wife by all five of the Pandava brothers, and how, subsequently, the rival group of princes led by cousin Duryodhana taunted Draupadi for this strange liaison, calling her a whore and making lewd suggestions that she oblige them as well. The incident led to Draupadi untying her hair, and vowing to leave it hanging loose till she had bathed it with the blood of the evil cousins.

From then on, a curtain of hair hangs over Draupadi's tale. Such a curtain of lustrous hair, we recall, was a gift of Yama, the lord of death, to the Devi. Like the Goddess, Draupadi too straddles an eighteen-day war with her heavy locks in disarray. The elders had kept quiet when she was dragged into the public gaze by her hair, so also the five great warriors she was expected to sleep with and be protected by. Revenge rustles and crackles in Draupadi's words, and in her shining unbraided tresses, like sparks that fly upwards.

♎   ♎   ♎

1988: Rupan Deol Bajaj was publicly pawed and humiliated. A senior officer of the Indian Administrative Services, she was assaulted at a party at a friend's house in Chandigarh, the capital of Punjab. She alleged that the police chief of the state had turned up drunk. According to a First Information Report filed by Rupan, he first made lewd suggestions to her, then slapped her bottom in full view of some fifty people, most of them the seniormost bureaucrats and journalists in the state. A hush fell on the party. Then some women murmured in consternation. But, as Rupan got up to leave, the tall, well-built police official is alleged to have barred her way menacingly. Rupan got away somehow and filed both a police report and also a case in a magisterial court.

Then the backlash began.

Reports were published in papers that said that the governor of the state, himself an eminent jurist, had refused to back Rupan. Some reports began referring to the case frivolously as the 'bottom-pinching case'. A senior columnist, a friend, they said, of the police chief, hinted in his columns that Rupan was actually the one that had been carrying a torch for the handsome police officer and when spurned, had given way to a hellish fury and filed the reports. The chief secretary in Punjab, the cabinet secretary in Delhi—none were willing to back a relatively junior official, and a woman at that, against a senior official who was talked about in awed tones as the Super Cop.

On October 12, 1995, seven years after the incident, the Supreme Court of India supported Rupan's right to prosecute the police chief.

She shall proceed to do just that, she says, and does.

Ω   Ω   Ω

Men let Draupadi down again and again while women counsel silence and compliance.

Draupadi wants neither counselling nor sympathy. She wants revenge. She wants her dignity reasserted. The only man Draupadi can confide in is her dear friend Krishna, the dark cowherd-turned-warrior, who always stands by women. Her faith in action and her disdain for passive philosophising links Draupadi inextricably with the dark God Krishna.

Restless and volatile, Draupadi shakes up everyone around her. All except Yudhisthir, the eldest of the Pandavas. Bhima, the middle brother, sides with her in principle but he dare not defy his mother and elder brother. Arjuna is busy womanising when he is not achieving feats in archery, and Nakul-Sahdeva, the twins, are enough company for each other. With five such husbands, it is no wonder that Draupadi does not want to be a married woman anymore.

'They are of no relation to me,' she confides disdainfully to Krishna.

Krishna tries to calm her with philosophy, but Draupadi does not wish to analyse her thoughts, beseech divine intervention or sit back calmly.

'You let us lose our riches as the lazy cowherd loses cows in the jungle. Fie upon your detachment! It is cowardice disguised as high principle. Do not think of renunciation or detachment. Either you win or you lose. What you attain through your labour is alone your own. Sitting in my father's lap, I've heard it said by a learned man, "He wo forgives each time, even his servants do not respect him." Timely action is what one needs. I've heard that the God of *dharma* protects if protected. Why are you then a toy in his hands? Gods are said to be like kind parents. But Brahma whips us with a lash. Why?'

Krishna looks at her sadly. He knows what Draupadi is talking about.

'Krishnaa', the dark woman, the second name fits Draupadi. Her dark saturnine features have never broken into a smile since she untied her tresses. Yet she has immense dignity. When in exile with her husbands, she cooks and serves the brothers and their mother quietly. She has a pot, given by her friend Krishna, which always has rice in it, till she has eaten. She is always the last to eat. When visitors come, she warms up rice and greens from the forest for them. She eats her own food indifferently, for in her mind, a fire burns all the time. Everything weighs on her: her humiliation in the court of the Kauravas, the long stay in the forest, the stint as a maid in King Virat's palaces. She never lets her husbands forget anything either. Her hair is to hang over their lives day and night, stinging like nettles. It is like a dark shroud over any possible happiness.

Ω   Ω   Ω

1995: She too was named Draupadi by her parents. But then they did not know she'd be reliving the original tragedy after these thousands of years. She grew upto be as bright and energetic as her namesake and was elected the Sarpanch, the head of her village panchayat of Sakore, in the district of Raigad in MP. On November 17, when the panchayat met to commemorate the birthday of India's late woman Prime Minister, Indira Gandhi, an altercation ensued. The other members of the panchayat stripped Draupadi and tried to gang-rape her publically. She escaped. Reports coming from her village say Draupadi Bai has not tied her hair in a bun since the incident, and has declared to the administration and also the chief minister of the state that she will put up her hair only when her molesters are caught, tried and jailed.

As Draupadi Bai roams the state, people are beginning to gather around her. They are already calling her molesters Duhshasana and Duryodhana, after the villains from the *Mahabharata* who had stripped the princess Draupadi.

Ω   Ω   Ω

1995: The Sikh widows, whose husbands were killed in the anti-Sikh riots of 1984 (after the assassination of Indira Gandhi at the hands of her Sikh bodyguards) have completed over a decade of widowhood. A survey report reveals unhealed scars. Several of them remarried close relatives after being widowed, but most of the marriages where the widow had children by her first husband, have broken up. The government grants and charity from religious organisations cover them only partly. Their fear and their memories of the days remain.

Their children are going wayward; pimps from red-light areas hang around enticing their pubescent daughters. Their sons are falling prey to the virus of terrorism and getting into trouble all the time.

Time, these women feel, is on the side of the criminals.

'I have faith in the One above,' the scrawny woman with dead eyes says. 'Those that widowed us shall also leave widows and children behind. There shall be no sound when His stick descends. Remember this.'

There is no mistaking those Draupadi eyes.

Ω   Ω   Ω

By the medieval period, the *Mahabharata* had been translated into the vernacular languages of the south, the oldest among them being Tamil. In the south, Draupadi's story merges, for millions of her Tamil devotees, into the tales about other great local Goddesses—Meenakshi of Madurai, Kamakshi of Kanchipuram and the androgynous Goddess of Tiruvannamalai, she, who roared at injustice and slayed the demon all by herself as the Gods quaked and cowered. To the epic mythology of Draupadi, a regional mythology gets further appended. As Draupadi Amman, the fiery *kanya* now gains two local guardians; Pottu Raja and Muttal Ravuttan. One is a Hindu, the other a Muslim (*Villiputtur Alvar's Tamil version of the* Mahabharata, *dated 14th century*). Outside Draupadi temples of South Arcot, usually stands the fierce-looking figure of Pottu Raja (king of buffaloes). As Pota Raju (Telugu) of Andhra, this demon is almost identical to Mahishasur—the buffalo demon of the Durga tales of the north. The only difference is that Pottu Raja is a contrite demon; a timely conversion to Draupadi Amman's cult saved his life. It is also said that a king, Cunitan of Kaushambi, lived five generations after Arjuna's great-grandson Janamejaya. One Pottu Raja was his minister. He accompanied the king to the Himalayas for a sacrifice. In the king's absence, demons attacked his kingdom, which was saved, along with his subjects, by the divine intervention of Draupadi as Parashakti, who emerged out of fire to slay the demons. The head of the last demon, she handed to Pottu Raja as a trophy. So to date, he stands at the door of her temples, holding the severed head.

History comes round to Draupadi's doorstep, begging for pardon, again and again. It stands at her door with severed heads dripping blood, heads of enemies who have refused to cow down. Draupadi smiles and forgives those that apologise. The heads of the fools drip and drip blood.

From Tamil Nadu to the Himachal Pradesh, Draupadi defeats time and makes the past unfurl like a chart. Nothing but nothing must be forgotten. Nothing that degrades women anywhere, must go unpunished. Draupadi is female memory, pitted against the static powers of the male state and its laws. She is Mahakali trampling Mahakali—Great Time itself. Whenever a just cause is threatened, she shall arise out of fire, as Veer Panchali, to act against those who perpetrate injustice.

Ω Ω Ω

Draupadi's end when it comes, is as dramatic as her birth.

At the end of the epic, and the carnage of the eighteen-day war which claims all their relatives and five of her sons, their sons and even an unborn child, Draupadi's peace-loving husband Yudhishthir leads the brothers and their common wife up north to do penance.

Why should Draupadi do penance for upholding the cause of justice, one may ask. But she goes, anyhow. And with her vilifiers all dead, she has nothing much left to live for anyway. She walks behind her five husbands. Not one of them can heal the angry wounds that are her eyes. They walk with averted faces. Draupadi follows, ever-dutiful but silent.

Day. Night. Dawn. Fatigue. Cold. Numbness. First, the green conifers are sighted. Then more and more woods. Then come the *bhoja* trees with bark smooth as paper, and finally, the *deodaru* forests, the timber of the Gods.

For Draupadi nothing matters anymore. Her eyes are dead already. She trudges on listlessly. She scarcely eats. Her skin cracks, heals and leaves scars. New scars merge with the old ones.

The sky fills with snow-bearing clouds. The sky empties. Draupadi trudges on. By the time the brothers sight the Himalayas, Draupadi has begun to falter in her steps. Unsteady as a fawn, she falls slowly. Then lies in the snow and closes her eyes. The brothers avert their faces. Draupadi dies before their penance begins. A row of hollow eyes watches her for a while. Then the men move on.

Draupadi dies as the lamp goes out at dawn. She had no use for the sun, nor for the summit. She has had her revenge.

Born of the fire, she breathes her last in the snow.

Kunti

While still a child, the young princess Pritha—later to be known as Kunti—had been given away by her parents to a childless uncle, to bring up as his own. The sage Durvasa, otherwise known for his fiery temper, was so pleased with her sweet temper, they say, that he blessed her with the powers of summoning up any God at her will and mating with him to produce a son.

A boon can beget foolhardy desires in the heart of a lonely young girl. A curious Kunti called upon the sun God. Come, Kunti whispered out of her window to the sun, come burn me. The slender teenaged virgin breathed in the bright air slowly at first, then eagerly, and the room was suddenly enkindled by a giant presence blazing first upon her threshold, then upon her body. It bared her, set her on fire, then solaced her, and quit at cock's crow. Precise as a clock.

An old story this. And timeless as Mahakali.

The sun God's bride for the night, Kunti quickened with his seed and became an unwed mother. Her first-born child, Karna, had to be put in a basket and floated down the river—what else? He was to be brought up by a lowly charioteer and his wife, and to grow into a sensitive, brilliant, but also wayward youth. By a mad coincidence, he was befriended by the evil Kaurava, Duryodhana, and became the sworn enemy of Kunti's legitimate sons. By another mad miracle, Kunti, the *kanya* became a virgin once again. Nobody blinked a lid as she was given in marriage to king Pandu, the jaundiced prince, he that was sired by the ugly poet Vyasa under cover of darkness and filth.

So much for legitimacy and perpetuating the male line.

Kunti's jaundiced husband, Pandu, turned out to be as impotent as his official father Vichitravirya was. A deer he had hunted down, it is said, had cursed him. Pandu, keen to beget male heirs to the throne, pleaded with Kunti with folded hands to produce a son by using her magical powers to summon a God who could impregnate her. The obliging wife Kunti did so, and bore him three sons.

First she called upon and mated with the God of *dharma* to produce Yudhishthir, then she mated with the wind god Vayu, to produce Bhim, and then with Indra to produce Arjuna.

Madri, the other wife of Pandu, was similarly helped by the virile Gods whom Kunti summoned for her, at her husband's suggestion. Madri mated with the divine physicians, the twin Ashwini Kumars, and produced the twins Nakul and Sahdev.

The five sons were known as the Pandavas—the sons of Pandu. Krishna referred to them as Kaunteya—sons of Kunti. Pandu died young, Vyasa says, when he tried to make love to Madri. The contrite Madri chose to immolate herself on her husband's pyre as penance for having led him on to the suicidal act. So the widow Kunti was left alone to bring up five fatherless boys in a family riddled with envy and rage.

She had one illegitimate son and five legitimate ones, none of whom were sired by their so-called father. And Kunti, the matriarch, was made to uphold the principles of patriarchy and paternal legitimacy.

She carried out the task with an astounding devotion. Like many Indian matriarchs, the idea of legitimacy had by now come to mean much to Kunti. She didn't let her sons forget that the Kauravas had acquired the throne by crooked means. Their father's throne was legitimately theirs, she told them again and again. She also inculcated in her sons the need to be led by their elder brother, the desire to obey him. Doubt was an unnecessary luxury for princes living in exile. The eldest had to lead by example. If violence was the need of the hour, he must eschew pacifism and shed blood. It was his *dharma*, she said. For patriarchy to acquire roots, the men must stay together, she said.

So Kunti taught the five brothers to assume

amiably didactic tones towards each other, and towards their mother maintain a marked attitude of deference. She did not whitewash or embellish Pandu, their perceived father. But she dared not talk about her illegitimate son—Karna—to anyone. Not until the swords were drawn and the legitimate ones were at a risk from the illegitimate one.

During their exile, Arjuna, her youngest and the most favourite son, brought home Draupadi. 'Mother, look what I got today,' Arjuna told his mother laughingly. Since the sons usually went out to hunt or beg for food, Kunti, without looking, said, 'You must divide it equally among all of you.' And when she realized her mistake, it was already too late. So it is said.

The fact is, the wise Kunti had read lust and longing in the eyes of the other sons. If the price for keeping the brothers together was to sacrifice Draupadi, so be it, she had decided.

The brothers, crazed by Draupadi's luminous beauty, agreed instantly to share her 'as per your wishes, Mother'.

Draupadi's fate was thus sealed.

♎ ♎ ♎

Shame is a mixed emotion in the *Mahabharata*.

Living in exile and penury, with her five sons married to one woman, shame is not what mothers like Kunti want to acknowledge. But shame is what the Kauravas want all proud women to bow to.

Shame is what Duryodhana wants Kunti to feel when he asks a whole retinue of snickering sages to go and feast in Kunti's forest cottage and its meagre kitchen.

Shame is when her menstruating daughter-in-law

Draupadi is dragged by the hair into the royal court, where her sons have lost her in a rigged game of dice to the Kauravas.

And the ultimate shame of all is when the mother has to sneak into her illegitimate son Karna's tent at night to tell him that she is his real mother, and will he please spare her legitimate sons? Karna agrees to spare all but Arjuna, his chief rival. 'You will still have five sons left, either way,' he says bitterly.

Kunti stands with bowed head for a while, then leaves as she came.

She doesn't attempt to embrace Karna, nor he her. The wounds run too deep on each side.

But shame rankles. It is a bitter, hollow and wry Kunti who remonstrates with a Brahmin who is about to bless Draupadi: 'If you must bless my daughter-in-law, please let her bear lucky children, not strong and learned ones such as mine. I brought to birth these powerful and erudite Pandavas, and look how they suffer in the forest.'

♎   ♎   ♎

Through centuries, Kunti, her flesh laid waste by days of fasting and living in the forests, has wandered the earth, with all those refugee tribes that have lost their moorings. Together they all loiter in strange no-man's-lands that scavengers have claimed. Here they all stop. They collect endlessly: bags, half-eaten food, roots, anything that can be sold, or worn or eaten. At night they sleep fitfully in dark corners, shooing away stray animals, protecting the children with only their frail bodies. They cling to near-obsolete rituals, songs and folk tales which shall become their legacy to their sons, dowry to their daughters. They know all about power and about losing it. They are beyond shame. While the sons sit, gulping down skimpy meals, the women wipe their eyes on the edge of their saris. Men have let them down all through their lives, yet it will always be to men that they'll turn for protection, and for guidance.

Such stubbornness. Such sorrow. Such shame.

♎   ♎   ♎

When his mother died, the writer-playwright Mohan Rakesh wrote a story called *Ardra*. It was about the 1947 Partition of India and Pakistan; about the refugees migrating from one part of Punjab to an alien land, and a mother that kept the family together even if she could not help them hold on to their sanity very well. Many said they recognised their own mothers in it. Mothers with soiled, old funereal clothes.

Mothers one loved but was deeply ashamed of.

Mothers that stood on the fringes of our dreams.

♎   ♎   ♎

The Singh family had prospered and prospered.

'Stay together,' our Sikh neighbour from Lahore would say again and again to her five sons: they of the tall and lean frames, thick hirsute faces and booming laughs. In August of 1947 when the country was partitioned and the communal carnage began, the family was forced to lock up their ancestral mansions in rural Punjab and migrate to the hills in India. It was rumoured that the old woman had left behind the holy book of the *Granth Sahib*, but contrived to bring with her a bag full of the family's gold, which had helped her 'settle' her sons.

It was a rough journey and a rougher landing. But at least they were together.

Once they reached India, they bought land. 'Buy land,' the mother urged them again and again, 'or else gold.' 'Nothing else lasts.' So they bought farms in the rich Terai area: houses in hill-stations. 'More!' the mother said. So they married girls from rich Punjabi families who also brought substantial dowries of gold, cash, land, houses, cars and sofa-sets covered in satin.

But gold, land and women, *zar*, *joru* and *zamin*, bring problems.

Once the daughters-in-law arrived, the sons began to change. They took to looking sheepish and acting restless. Finally, they confessed to their misgivings. The old woman's fury knew no bounds. A partition of the family? 'How can blood brothers part company? Haven't you heard of Lord Rama's words when his brother was hurt—"You may find another wife but not a brother born out of your own mother's womb." I know who is putting you upto it.'

Biji stood resolutely against the tide of family displeasure. She withstood the nights that beckon a man and take him away from his mother's side. She guarded against her sons' escape like a night-warden and kept them all under one roof. She cried, she fainted, she fasted, she told stories incessantly of the tradition of vows, of familial pride. During the summer she summoned them all to the hills. Here, they all hung about, cracked jokes, bragged, then sank into moody depressions, stealing up staircases and banging doors on their private misery.

One had seldom known a more miserable family, nor a better-run business empire. Their farms and fields bloomed as the five brothers worked together. But misery multiplied as their women bickered.

Finally, the wives withered away into bland middle age, knitting pullovers and ushering in their own daughters-in-law. Slowly, they agreed with Biji, the old mother. It was good to be together. Biji beamed as she gathered the brood around her at her death-bed: 'Have sons,' she blessed all her grand-daughters. 'Daughters and birds fly away. Sons and gold and land stay with you,' she said as she lay dying.

Ω   Ω   Ω

The sea breeze was warm on our balcony. Our guest, Biji's son, was now an eminent economist. He was known for his fixed smile and iron-clad will. There was that moment when he thawed just for a couple of minutes as he saw, in the balcony across, an old woman bent over a sewing machine. 'That is how Biji brought us up after the Partition,' he said. 'We'd lost everything but she managed to send us to good schools. She brought me books from the British Council Library once, and it began to rain. She wrapped her own *dupatta* around the books, and caught a chill. She died a week later—lung congestion.'

The son's memory preserved Biji, but like a fossil. When the political scene altered and his government broke firm contracts, he blacked out his own reports and swallowed his convictions so he could be appointed to another top slot in a faraway land. Each government needed liars with honeyed tongues. For the time being, he survived—and prospered.

Ω   Ω   Ω

The world of Kunti. A world of black migrations, of broken words, betrayals, and parting of friends. Its ethical boundaries keep shifting, for in a war nothing holds true for long. The world around becomes a counterworld to that one was taught to function in, but she, Kunti, does not run away. She tries to cope in the only way she knows. She makes it possible for her sons to survive in chaos, but in doing so she often leads families and nations into deadly wars against one another. Kunti may live on till the end of the civil war, but by the time death claims her, in her heart she has already been dead for several years.

Mandodari

Mandodari. The name means 'she of the slight waist'. This beautiful, proud and fearless woman became the wife of the demon king Ravana, because her father, Maya the great architect, in the manner of most Hindu fathers, was in a hurry to get rid of a daughter. 'Being a father to a daughter,' said he, 'is a misery to any man who seeks honour'. (*Ramayana 8.12.11*). So Maya gave away his daughter to Ravana even though he knew of the terrible curse that shrouded the demon king's birth. His ostensible excuse was that he had a great respect for Ravana's paternal grandfather (*8.12.20-21*). Lineage, a man's ancestry, was to Maya more precious than rubies.

Ω   Ω   Ω

As young girls, we were told and retold the tale about a certain grand-aunt whose well-to-do father had married his young daughter off into a family known chiefly for its indigence. 'The ground,' he said by way of explanation, 'sinks seven fingers each time a daughter is born, fourteen spans each time she menstruates in her father's house. The boy may not have money, but he has an excellent lineage, and an early marriage is a good thing.' Having done the deed, he almost forgot about his daughter till, one day, business took him to the village she lived in. Having gone that far, the father decided to pay his daughter a visit. When he reached her hut, he saw her sitting patiently stirring a pot in which she was roasting pebbles mixed with a fistful of grain to pacify her hungry waiting children.

'What are you cooking, my girl?' the father asked, appalled by the sight.

'What I'm cooking, Father, is our lineage. This is what I roast and eat each day,' the daughter replied, turning away to hide her tears.

With fathers and husbands like that, is it any wonder women believe in Kali, wild and fierce, untameable and unforgiving?

♎   ♎   ♎

Like most unwanted children, Mandodari is sharp, perceptive and forthright in pointing out injustice. 'Untimely death does not visit men for no reason. Sita is the reason you shall die,' she says bluntly to husband, Ravana, who had abducted the exiled prince Rama's wife by force. It is not Rama's might but the wronged woman, Sita's curse, that shall be her husband's undoing, Mandodari prophesies, correctly as it turned out. 'The destruction of the leaders of your clan will be a result of your anger and lust. The tears of chaste women do not fall to the ground to be absorbed and forgotten. They bring results.'

Round her palace, Mandodari erects a barricade of frosty exclusivity. The vulgar motley crowd is free to visit her husband, not his mutinous and orthodox wife.

Majestic in her rage, sorrow, wisdom and piety curdle like sour milk in her breast. She stands just out of her husband's reach, waiting for his end as her dire prophecy comes true. Then Mandodari burns herself on her husband's pyre.

Mandodari's history creeps through the ages into the darkness of countless homes where children sleep innocently, curled like foetuses, and wives lie awake, waiting for the adulterous husbands' returning steps to the outside bedroom, wishing them dead.

Tara

Tara, the wife of the monkey king Bali, is a man's woman. She survives the injustice of her situation sometimes by her wits, at others by feminine wile.

Men of a family stay close, and brothers must not kill and grab from each other, is Tara's firm belief. She was first married to Bali, who died but returned unexpectedly to life. By then Tara had been claimed by Bali's twin brother Sugriva, as his wife. She returned to her first husband but an unappeased Bali now snatched Sugriva's wife, Ruma, in revenge.

The battle-lines were drawn.

Like Mandodari, Tara first urged Bali to return Ruma to Sugriva. Like Ravana, Bali refused. But unlike Mandodari, Tara's objections now turned to concern. She had been gifted with the knowledge of rare *mantras*. So Tara performed the protective rites (*Swastyayana*) for Bali and sent him to fight a duel with Sugriva. She is said, however, to have wrested a promise from Bali that he would not kill his own brother. Unfortunately, one of them was doomed to die anyway. Bali did not kill Sugriva, but Sugriva's mentor Rama, hid behind a tree and wounded Bali mortally. The dying Bali gave Tara as wife to Sugriva·

and said to his contrite brother, 'Always go with Tara's advice. It never goes without effect (*4.22.13-14, Ramayana*).'

Queen Tara, the natural-born diplomat, went on to step aside when Rama's emissary, Hanuman, suggested that her young son from Bali, Angad, be crowned king and she rule as dowager. She did not deny her ability to rule, but said demurely: 'That duty now devolves upon his uncle Sugriva.'

Tara understood male vanity. By leaving the question of succession to the guilt-ridden uncle's conscience, she ensured that the throne went to her son after Sugriva, without hard words or bloodshed. Tara was to pour oil over troubled waters once again when Sugriva took to merrymaking as king and neglected his duty to Rama—that of raising an army of monkeys to fight the demon king Ravana. As Laxmana, the fiery young brother of Rama came to rebuke Sugriva, Tara is herself said to have gone to the gates to pacify the young prince. Tara waited till his expected outburst was over, then gently chided Laxmana for rushing to false conclusions about her Sugriva. 'Anyone denied pleasures and driven into penury has a right to indulge himself when he has won them back,' she said, quoting examples of several austere sages, who, too, when their rigorous meditational exercises were over, gave them themselves upto the pleasures of the flesh for a while. She had, moreover, she confided to Laxman at this point, already taken care of everything. 'Things have been so well-arranged,' said she, 'that all the monkeys recruited by the Mighty one are gathered here today. Why do you wish to frighten the already decimated womenfolk of the palaces unnecessarily?'

Laxmana, abashed at her words, immediately asked Sugriva for his forgiveness for his rudeness

(*4.36.20*) and praised Tara as a woman endowed with rare talents.

Ω   Ω   Ω

Centuries before the World Wars and the Internet, Tara understands about deadlines and corporate warfare. She will not nag nor bully, nor take to pleading feminine frailty. She is a woman with her feet planted firmly on the ground, determined against giving in to dreams. Tara knows that when all escape routes behind are blocked, people must escape forward. Anger is a luxury the weak can ill afford. She talks sweetly even to those that have killed her husband, and now threaten the new one. She presents her case so even a fool may see how it helps everyone to help her. And when reconciliation comes, she accepts it with a gracious inclination of her head and a smile.

Ω   Ω   Ω

Ahilya, Draupadi, Kunti, Tara and Mandodari.

Behind these five names chanted with such devotion each morning is a sinister message for women.

What do these five lives reveal? Well, according to the prevailing wisdom of our popular culture and the Right Wing parties in India, there is only one answer: it was their struggle to align with truth that caused these women so much pain. They were unhappy precisely because they tried to be truthful and free. And their victories had always to be pyrrhic ones.

They gained control over their husbands' minds and their clans, only to destroy them. Ergo, women, if they are to live happily, must look away when truth beckons.

It is a view that repeatedly finds a ready berth in our media. In popular regional films and television soaps, emancipated working women pay for their freedom with empty beds; empty nests. The Sunday colour supplements of newspapers peddle articles by columnists doubling as self-appointed social analysts. They too claim that women can't have it all. They underplay the rise in the graphs of crimes against women, and highlight the slight rise in crimes committed by women.

But myths breathe different secrets for story-tellers as they forage for them in damp family vaults. The poets Vyasa and Valmiki have documented unique human struggles for truth and justice where good human beings may be victimized, stifled and oppressed, but never silenced. Ahilya, Kunti, Tara, Draupadi and Mandodari must be asked to lend us their tenacity, and their rage, so we may comment on our travesty of democracy, on caste-based reservations, on globalisation and labour laws, all of which burn women on funeral pyres and then look beyond the flames and the rancid smoke and chant, '*Sati Mata Ki Jai*! May our glorious, self-negating mothers live long!'

These women present to us a balance-sheet of human history; the sum total of those hushed secrets our young girls have pondered as they've lain on string-cots in the open, staring at the meagre sky above and all those nameless stars. Elegant and austere, these women accompany our history wherever it goes, entering women's dreams, walking along old tracks by abandoned towns and factories, holding their sisters' hands in theirs. Calloused, but free hands.

✹

Epilogue

'*Junho*? (May I go please?),' queries the timid voice of the daughter-in-law bird in the Uttarakhand forests.

'*Bhol! Bhol!* (Tomorrow! Tomorrow!),' orders the mother-in-law, another bird-call, grim and stern, uttered in mid-flight.

Their men having migrated to the plains, this hapless old woman and her daughter-in-law, the legend runs, were forced to subsist on a diet of berries dried in the sun. Spring came. Married girls began to go on visits to their parents' homes. Each day, the daughter-in-law would see her friends leave and would ask if she too could go see her parents, and eat the *kafal* fruit that grew in their yard. But the mother-in-law would bark: '*Bhol!*'

If she, the younger one, went away, who would climb the trees and shake the branches to bring the berries down?

'*Bhol!*' she repeated. '*Bhol!*' Again and again.

Hunger or loneliness—or perhaps both—killed the two women ultimately, and the duo, legend says, then turned into two birds, ceaselessly crying out to each other through the centuries.

The little blackbird hops upon the *kafal* trees and begins to wail—'Ah, the *kafal* berries are ripe, and I didn't get to taste them (*Kafal pakko, mail ni chakho!)'*,then cocks her head and pleads, '*Junho?*'

'*Bhol,*' answers the mother-in-law's faint voice from somewhere deep within the dark heart of the forest. '*Bhol!*'

♎   ♎   ♎

Dark *kafal* berries glisten upon the branches like tumescent nipples. The young women wait for a '*Bhol!*' that shall never come.

♎   ♎   ♎

Welcome to the no-man's-land where Goddesses roam freely, disguised as *kanyas*, as prostitutes, vendors, beggars and penniless heads of families. Where each mouthful of food is sacred and it is a sin to waste even a grain of salt. Where you must get up each morning and clean your mouth with a twig of bitter *neem*, and greet the male forest officer, without whose permission you cannot use the *neem*.

♎   ♎   ♎

The road runs for miles as we bump past farms, villages and cities, thickly peopled—and owned always by men.

'What do you mean, married women must have the same land-rights as their brothers?' the beetle-browed director of the prestigious Gokhale Institute of Pune asks me with ill-concealed irritation. 'Women marry and move in with their in-laws. How can they carry paternal land with them? Our tradition, in Punjab, is to give them a dowry, not land.'

'Land is what we are dying for,' Govindamna from Kanchipuram district in Tamil Nadu tells a group of women sent to investigate a government report on the area. She has five children and a husband to support. She manages to live on seasonal work in paddy fields for which she earns ten rupees a day, when there is work. When there is drought there is no work for the likes of her and they starve and wait. She cannot get her over-fertile womb sterilized, she grumbles, because the lady-doctor at the city-hospital says her heart is weak. What about the husband then? Can't he get himself sterilized? Govindamna looks at the questioner sadly and shakes her head, 'We cannot ask him to, Amma, he is the head of the family. He supports us!'

☊   ☊   ☊

The border between the lives of owners and dependents in our country is not marked because it does not need to be. As you cross it you realize immediately that you've entered a different world. One by one, lines that divide, demarcate and codify property and power begin to fade away. Paths begin to go not forward, but in spirals that may plunge and soar suddenly. There are no fences between homes and pavements, between goats and children, dogs and pigs. Here they all wander about freely in search of work, of food. But work is seasonal and so is food. Off-season, everyone turns into a predatory collector: of cow-dung, plastic bags, medicinal herbs, firewood, *neem* twigs, gum, honey, pine-cones. Hands and feet claw, scratch and slash to grab and to survive. All that is acquired is sold then to traders who come from outside and who in their turn sell it to others for fifty or even hundred times more.

This, the outer circle of no-man's-land, is a dark one. Restless Kali; blood-thirsty Chhinnamasta: beady-eyed Dhoomravati with her withered old dugs; these are the Goddesses who hover on its peripheries. They are all dark-skinned with hollowed faces and burning eyes. You can see them in the shape of a blackbird, a weeping river or in the power of a stone, a sickle, a muscular coconut-fibre cord or an axe with a firm grip.

It is hard to get outsiders to recognise the glimpses of the Goddess that flash suddenly upon fibrous wrists and corded necks, as women desperately strain to lop off that last branch and scoop up that last mound of steaming hot dung.

Ω Ω Ω

The Ibrahimpura Taluka Agricultural Labour Union has ten thousand members. About fifty women members had come to the meeting to discuss the problems of bonded labourers in the area: 'We may be landless,' their local leader Pochamma said, 'yet we know about land-reform Acts. We see around us all this fertile land occupied by landowners, and we think, "Why is it not so for us, bonded labourers?" '

The women applied for permission to acquire fifty acres of government land, of which there was a great deal around. No action was taken on this petition. Finally, they occupied the land by force and began clearing it so that they could plant crops. But, that was not to be.

One morning, as these women were working for their landlords in an orchard of custard apples, the police arrived, with one lady-officer. The women were brutally beaten. Their clothes were ripped off. Some were even dragged around by their hair. Pochamma's daughter-in-law had just had a baby, so she begged that the young mother, at least, should not be beaten. The police made Pochamma lift her daughter-in-law's sari to confirm her condition, and satisfied, arrested Ponchamma instead. Her skinny, wrinkled sixty-year-old's thighs remained bruised for a long time. In her eyes, anger burnt dark and hot: 'Can we not till land? Can't the police be punished for torturing women? Is the landlord God, that he can do what he likes?'

Does Pochamma believe in a divinity? She does, she says. Her sorrows keep her faith alive. 'So many sorrows I have been through', she says. 'Who but the Goddess could have helped me survive?'

Sometimes you need just one person to dig out a buried belief.

Male or female, there are few journalists who visit these devasted cremation grounds of Kali surrounding the no-man's-land. Those that have built comfortable homes and have their own fertile lands, cannot bear to look at these bleak Hiroshima contours. When they do go come here with their cameras and writing pads, they are sure to make their escape soon. Later they go on to make allusions and insinuations about women of their own class and kind—those, who like them, have power. Aren't our women's groups ashamed of such poverty, they ask angrily. Their anger hides a deep guilt, and of course, a lack of patience. Kali's is a land that tests patience, and, of course, faith.

Sometimes you need just one article to demolish a faith.

Sometimes you need just one Pochamma to restore it.

Ω   Ω   Ω

Gouri Amma is a woman of the Kasthal Kapo caste from Andhra Pradesh who cremates bodies at the Harish Chandra burning *ghat* at Kharagpur, near Calcutta. She is, she says, perhaps the only woman in the profession. Gouri Amma's family came from Palasa, a little village in the southern state of Andhra Pradesh, when she was only ten. That was thirty years ago. Now she is a forty-year-old widow with three daughters, whom she has married off with her earnings as a cremator. She earns around a thousand to fifteen hundred rupees a month and is proud of her profession. 'I'm earning an honest living, at least,' she declares. Her only sorrow, she says, is that when her husband Kakulu died, she was too poor to spend the three hundred rupees required for a decent cremation, so she buried him instead, after digging his grave herself.

'Each morning I sit beside his grave,' she says, and cry and apologise to him for even though I am a cremator, I could not cremate him. I had to save money for the girls' weddings, see?' But she thinks Kakulu has forgiven him because the sapling she had planted at the head of his grave has grown into a young tree and nods its branches whenever she sits under it and says her prayers.

A temple to Goddess Kali guards the gates of her crematorium.

Ω   Ω   Ω

As one enters deeper into Goddess-land, one begins to see tall and straight-backed women with pitchers balanced impossibly on their graceful heads. There is, in their gait, a certain desire to dig in their heels and stay in a land where they belong even after the men choose to migrate to towns. The police visit this area frequently, to beat up, drag, disrobe and rape the challengers. They are put on trucks and driven away to police thanas. Some of them never return. Sometimes, bodies are discovered floating in some canal or hanging in a cell. The police call it suicide.

How and why do these women still rise and raise their voices, one wonders again and again.

Perhaps Ponchamma spoke the truth when she said that she only knew that she had to protest, she didn't know why. Her own family of bonded labourers had all worked meekly for their landlords for generations for a pittance: a few measures of paddy and an old sari. No one had ever rebelled or thought of a *Karma* other than the one they were born into.

Was it her parents' acquiescence that had spawned Pochamma's Draupadi-like rebellion? Or was she conceived to voice a protest her parents could not utter? Who filled her head with such improbable ideas?

Who knows?

Ω   Ω   Ω

There was no mistaking the Draupadi eyes. Katori Devi carried memories of her humiliation everywhere with her, like a black shawl. Justice, she felt sure, would shine clean and clear one day, like the ringing of the bells around the Goddess' neck. In the meanwhile, she waited. In 1982, she, a forty-four-year-old lady teacher, went and sat in a protest *dharna* in front of the UP state Assembly in Lucknow. Few, including Katori Devi herself, knew that for fourteen years thereafter, she'd sit forlorn in a torn tent that housed a broken cot, a dirty bed-roll and documents regarding her case.

The case, according to newspaper reports, was as follows. In 1970, when Katori Devi was thirty-two years old, she was transferred out of her school in Mathura where she was the principal. When she protested, she was first sacked, then reinstated, but as punishment for her defiance, she was transferred from one small town to another for the next ten years. In 1981, she was physically assaulted by her tenant, and when she protested, was beaten up by the police. She then felt enough was enough and decided to stage a protest in front of the police station. The police were furious and arrested her. A custodial rape was attempted to terrorise her further and the arrest also cost Katori her job. After she lost her job and her faith in the police, Katori decided to go and sit in front of the state Assembly till the wrong done to her was avenged, no matter how long it took. It took fourteen years, and an impending election that made a big to-do about the women's 'vote-bank', for her case to be noticed by the state. At the end of February 1996, the state government of UP restored her services with retrospective effect from 1981 and granted her a two-year extension, the seniority due to her, a free bus pass (normally given to freedom fighters) and Rs 3.25 lakh as compensation for the lapsed service period. Disciplinary action against the policemen who had assaulted and arrested her for no reason, was also ordered.

The Governor who was then in charge of the state (three earlier elected governments having fallen for one reason or another in mid-term) was a crusty old politician with close ties with a major party. It was suggested in media reports that he may have been utilizing his gubernatorial powers to win over the

women's vote bank in favour of his party, to help it
to come to power in the state. He was banking, the
reports said, on recent public memory when women
from the hill region were assaulted and humiliated
by men of the rival party. He was, he said, at a
public function held to honour Katori Devi, full of
admiration for her Gandhian beliefs and her non-
violent protest against injustice.

Katori Devi, who was denied a hearing and
hounded for fourteen long years by all kinds of
governments, said nothing of course. She just joined
her palms by way of expressing her gratitude.

In our political rivers, made turgid by the general
elections, cases such as Katori's turn up every five
years like stray half-burnt corpses. At other times,
police excesses are not usually regarded as violations
of human rights by the authorities. They are, at
worst, treated as offences committed in the heat of
the moment, to be tried under the police's own laws.
And usually, the result is that the offenders are
transferred to another police station. If ever there is
a dismissal, reinstatement is quick to follow. What
women say does not scratch the surface of the
system, when offences committed against them are
tried.

But election time is different.

♎   ♎   ♎

She had married a minor politician, my favourite
teacher, I mean.

'Why haven't you married?' I had asked her
earlier. She was fiftyish and fading quietly into the
background of her land, and well-to-do family. 'Well,
all my life, I was very foolishly looking for a quiet
man who would listen to me,' she replied with a
twinkle.

Then suddenly, we heard that she had married this fast-talking, flashy young man some twenty years her junior. She died two years after that. It was rumoured that the ageing heiress' sudden death was perhaps not due to natural causes. The family hushed up the matter, of course. The young man inherited a lot and, one supposes, lived in comfort ever after.

One heard that on his late wife's death anniversary, he gave a lavish feast to a number of Brahmins, and tipped them heavily at the end of it all.

It was, again, an election year, as my mother pointed out. And it gave a politician a good image to celebrate his dead wife's *shraddha* in style.

If nothing else, at least her poor soul would be propitiated, other women in the family said, and we left it at that.

$$\Omega \qquad \Omega \qquad \Omega$$

You ask me what I mean by this story? What does it have to do with the Goddesses? Why bring her up in this connection? I ask you, what would *you* do if each story you picked up, that had a woman in it, pricked at your mind with unanswered questions? If under stories about women you felt there was something nameless but recognizable hiding and burrowing in the moist dark soil of the tales? Would you not try to understand who or what it was? Sita? Kakulu's body? My teacher? My friends X and Vijaya? Do you, like me, not feel inclined to find the answer even though you know that it can't sustain itself on the satiny surface of a language that has replaced the rough alphabets of your mother-tongue?

You cannot spew out Vac from your system any more than you can look away from Kali's bloodied hands. You cannot forget the headless Chhinnamasta, drinking her own blood, without remembering so many women.

Pochamma, Bhanwari, Rupan Deol, Badi Amma and my mother. Kali, Draupadi, Laxmi and Saraswati. None of them ever leave you.

Ω   Ω   Ω

Goddess country is dangerous country for writers. Here women teeter between life and death, between jobs and retrenchments, between hunger and hope, while men roam the area itching for wild fights and sex.

In this circle was born one of my last stories, the story of Shompa. She was widowed at the age of twenty and, along with her baby, was pushed out of the house by her in-laws. Entered at this point, Nikhil, a fellow-villager, who promised her a maid's job in the big rich city of Calcutta, and Shompa saw the chance she'd been waiting for. She left the baby in her sister-in-law's care, with the promise of sending her money regularly.

Eventually, Shompa, like thousands of other poor young women, landed in the red-light district of Calcutta. But she did not go under. Her shrewd mind, sturdy peasant's body and her great sense of humour helped her get the better of an abysmal situation. Today, she proudly declares that she runs her own place and collects 'rent' from her 'tenants'. Her daughter has been happily married off with a substantial dowry Shompa arranged for her. Back in Shompa's village, everyone, she says, knows what her profession is, even though everyone pretends to believe her when she says she's a maid.

'Hit them on the head with a silver shoe, Ma,' she says, 'and they all coo how right you are!' Her booming laugh sprays her bosom with red grains of betelnut. Her breasts bob up and down as she chortles.

'To live here,' Shompa says, 'you have to be strong and direct. If you show weakness and offer them your shoulder to sit on, they'll soon be urinating in your ear!'

Shompa understands with complete clarity the man-made rules of the world of money and the flesh trade. She trafficks between their world and others' with ease.

Shompa has covered herself and plugged her ears tight.

Right outside this tinsel-covered world of money and violence where Shompa lives, there is an unending row of book-stalls. This is where the world of the *bhadralok*—the cultured folk begins. Most of the kiosks are lending libraries that have been built with material purloined from abandoned sidings and building sites. The kiosks are windows into the heart of a secret world—the world of the urban poor who have nothing but their honour and a basic education to rely on. Here, books and periodicals are sold second, third and fourth-hand, until they fall apart and are then painstakingly rebound with thick needles and a sticky, home-made paste of flour and water that imparts an unpleasant fishy smell to the printed word.

♌ ♌ ♌

Our Badi Amma, after she put away her half-written stories, had started the first lending library in Vishnupur, in a tin shed in her garden.

Many still wondered how and why she did not make good her early promise? She was the last person you'd expect to meet in that strange, small, dimly-illuminated town of Vishnupur. But intellectuals, musicians and painters who wandered into this *bustee* on an impulse, and met up with her, found her extraordinarily attractive in a strange sort of way, because she could talk knowledgeably about almost anything—local flora and fauna, the traditional practices of weaving and spinning of wool, the making of woollen *namdas* and low-cost toilets. There they sat, in her over-furnished red and green wooden house, making polite talk with this woman with eyes like balls of fire who could quote great philosophers and historians that had visited her over the years, and made it all seem so normal, so easy.

To hear Badi Amma speak of the life around her, was to skip over the despair and defeat that cover the surface of most married lives like dust. As she talked of her cows and their milk-yields and recited Kalidasa, her guests, who came from all over for the two summer months in Vishnupur, entered a strange underworld of dreamy truths half told and seldom glimpsed. She spoke simultaneously of meals she had cooked and grand suppers served in her house, of the great classics she had read out to her grandfather at his behest, and the grand theories he had mysteriously revealed to her through the simplest gestures.

Like Prithvi's strange treasures, those that she had carried underground when she'd felt threatened and neglected, in Badi Amma's talk facts were often deliberately glossed over and then dangled tantalizingly before our senses and then hidden again. Her tales were like the moist peat of Vishnupur's verterinary hospital, where grasses were preserved for winter fodder for cows. Her secrets, also preserved in the shape of stories for precocious children, held the truth as she alone had glimpsed it in the life around her. During those long, frozen winter nights when the family warmed itself by the fireside, the stories thawed and flowed. And in summer, they bloomed and bloomed.

♎   ♎   ♎

Badi Amma is the Mahadevi enthroned in the very heart of the literary no-man's-land where women roam as Goddesses. She is the Gangotri from which all my tales flow, gurgling, happy and wayward, or unhapy and sullen.

As she laughed, scolded, schemed, sweated and cooked, Badi Amma let me see how ultimately the heart of every story—like the heart of a human being—must remain a supreme mystery. The awe and gratitude one feels when faced with this indubitable truth is the only thing that makes life worth living, and stories worth listening to.

Badi Amma surfaces in my tales at many places, suddenly and for no reason. She may appear in a certain look, a whispered aside, an angry roar, a coquettish smile, or a smart stinging slap upon the lewd wrist of a faceless molester.

Sometimes she appears in strange news reports, like the following.

♎   ♎   ♎

In the month of August 1995, villagers in Mayachar, a small hamlet on the banks of the Rupnarayan river in West Bengal, found a raft made of banana plants, decorated with a new bedsheet, colourful mats and flowers. A mosquito-net hung over the raft on four poles. On the raft lay the rotting corpse of a young bride decked in a red sari. The local fisherman, who found the strange vessel, also found a letter that said that the young bride was from the village Kholachali, and had died of snakebite. Since the village had no *ojha* who could cure her with holy incantations, her family were setting the body adrift down the river. If the raft were to reach a village that had an *ojha* who had learnt the *mantras* from Kamluk Kamakhya (in Assam), famous for its shamans and mystics, he could definitely bring her back to life, just as in the ancient legend of Behula and Lakhinder, Lakhinder had been restored to life by his wife's faith coupled with the *ojha's* magic words.

One of the fishermen said such bizarre cases were rare but did surface from time to time in the river waters. Why, before this there was the body of Jyotsna, the daughter of the snake-charmer, and before her, that of a ten-year-old boy from the village of Bargram. And before all of them, of course, there was Devi Behula with her Lakhinder.

There being no pucca roads in the area, the river is the only conduit, and it is where the bodies must surface, year after year. Also, one realizes, legends and hope and faith.

'You only have to be lucky,' said a fisherman's wife. 'Supposing one day you did reach a Learned One, then you could be restored to life. There is no doubt about that.'

What is it that the villagers along the Rupnarayan river—and all other rivers and valleys of India—think, as they lovingly anoint the bodies of their dead ones with sandalwood paste and flowers and set them adrift? What is it that moves the fishermen and women who encounter these rafts when they get caught in mounds of silt, to gently ease them out again into the current?

We will never know. Perhaps they do not know themselves. But one can feel the conviction in their sweeping gestures and strong vernacular assertions.

Ω   Ω   Ω

At the age of seventy-four, when Badi Amma lay dying, she too had inexplicably asked for fragrant flowers to be heaped around her: *mogra, sone, juhi, champa, chameli, parijata.* 'They remind me of the smell from the Devi's temple we used to visit in the hills,' she said to one in particular.

It was easy for members of her family to point out that she was never inclined to follow known rituals anyhow, unlike her sisters, suitably married and acclaimed by society as good, temple-going wives and mothers. It was easy for people to point out what she should have done and didn't. The roads she should not have taken, but did. 'Why does she want all this, why?' they asked each other again and again as they carried out her last wishes anyhow. And also prayed that she depart.

All through this litany of sounds, Badi Amma stared at the ceiling with her sightless eyes and smiled a beatific smile as her senses extracted the fragrance from the flower, the legend from fear, death from life.

And then she was gone.